MY EXPERIENCE WITH THE ULTIMATE TRUTH ABOUT
KUNDALINI

SHASHTRIA PRETTO

INDIA • SINGAPORE • MALAYSIA

Copyright © Shashtria Pretto 2025
All Rights Reserved.

ISBN
Paperback 979-8-89673-436-9
Hardcase 979-8-89699-302-5

This book has been published with all efforts taken to make the material error-free after the consent of the author. However, the author and the publisher do not assume and hereby disclaim any liability to any party for any loss, damage, or disruption caused by errors or omissions, whether such errors or omissions result from negligence, accident, or any other cause.

While every effort has been made to avoid any mistake or omission, this publication is being sold on the condition and understanding that neither the author nor the publishers or printers would be liable in any manner to any person by reason of any mistake or omission in this publication or for any action taken or omitted to be taken or advice rendered or accepted on the basis of this work. For any defect in printing or binding the publishers will be liable only to replace the defective copy by another copy of this work then available.

"No part of this publication may be reproduced, stored in a retrieval system, or transmitted in any form or by any means - electronic, mechanical, photocopying, recording, or otherwise - without the prior written permission of the copyright holder. This includes the content, design and cover page of this book"

Email: shashtriapretto21@gmail.com
Website: shashtriapretto.in

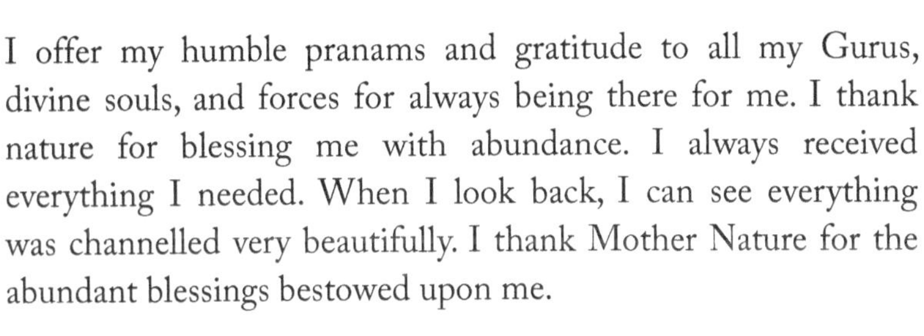

I offer my humble pranams and gratitude to all my Gurus, divine souls, and forces for always being there for me. I thank nature for blessing me with abundance. I always received everything I needed. When I look back, I can see everything was channelled very beautifully. I thank Mother Nature for the abundant blessings bestowed upon me.

Contents

About the Author

Shashtria Pretto (Sruthi) was born in 1974 and brought up in Mumbai. She is a deeply spiritual and compassionate Soul who has journeyed through life with an extraordinary blend of high acceptance, gratitude, and devotion. Her unwavering trust in Divine and profound spiritual experiences have shaped a path filled with miracles, wisdom, and a higher calling to inspire others.

One of Sruthi's most remarkable qualities is her ability to accept life as it unfolds, embracing every challenge and blessing with equal grace. Her life is a testament to her steadfast faith, as she navigated adversities without self-pity or glorification, always guided by divine presence. Her deep-rooted acceptance of people, situations, and the will of Divine reflects her belief in the perfection of life's design.

Her journey is profoundly spiritual, marked by encounters with celestial beings, divine energies, and great masters. From Lord Krishna and Lord Shiva to Lord Buddha, Lord Jesus, and many other gods, saints, and sages, Sruthi has been blessed with visions and interactions that transcend ordinary perception. These encounters have enriched her life and reinforced her purpose of spreading hope, healing, and inspiration to those around her.

A gifted healer, Sruthi has channelled divine energies to restore balance and wellness, touching the lives of people, animals, and even plants. Her ability to connect intuitively with the higher realms has enabled her to bring solace and transformation, profoundly impacting those she helps. Her experiences reaffirm her belief that miracles are real and achievable through alignment with divine grace and truth.

Her divinely guided and profoundly introspective book is a spiritual beacon for those seeking hope and higher meaning. Through her words, she shares the timeless wisdom and extraordinary experiences that define her journey, inspiring readers to overcome challenges, stay true to themselves, and embrace Divine within.

With an unwavering commitment to virtuous living, humility, self-effort, and service, Sruthi continues to be a source of light and inspiration. Her life exemplifies the power of acceptance, love, and divine connection, guiding others to explore their own paths to enlightenment and inner peace.

The Author's real name is Shashtria. The name Sruthi you see in the book is the name given to her by her Guru, an enlightened master. He has initiated hundreds of students into Kundalini Meditation but Sruthi is the only chosen one, whom he renamed, verbally. He told her Sruthi means revelation.

About the Book

This book truly narrates my life's journey and comes from divine guidance. Its contents are as complete as permissible under Divine approval and are a true account of a series of experiences, each transformational in its own way.

The main purpose of this work is to record the multitude of beautiful and divine experiences that I had by leading the right way of life, a higher spiritual journey.

Some of the finer yet unknown aspects of my life were revealed to me during this book's writing; for that, I feel blessed and grateful.

After multiple Kundalini awakenings and various higher spiritual experiences that accompany such awakenings, I can confidently say that oneness with our highest self is indeed possible under the guidance of a highly evolved Guru, only with complete dedication, discipline, and tenacity to follow a virtuous way of life.

My experiences might not be relatable to some and might seem out-of-this-world. My quest is to share them with my readers who believe in my fascinating journey, which I have been fortunate to experience and embrace.

Miracles and healing are for people who think and believe in a world outside of this world, in alternate mediums, divine energies, and the power of meditation.

My encounters and meetings with different deities are not mere visualizations, but what I have seen and been guided about. These celestial high-level beings choosing me is a pure and ethereal experience, and a shower of blessings upon me.

I was guided to write this book, and I wrote it by sharing what I have been guided to share. I was shown in meditation how the book's front cover should look. It was in different shades of blue, like waves of the sea in layers, from deep blue at the top, becoming lighter in shade towards the bottom. I was shown two names for the title of the book. I chose, "My Experiences With The Ultimate Truth About Kundalini."

This book is intended to inspire and motivate readers across the globe to overcome their life challenges while still maintaining their truth intact and not giving up on life and all the hope and promise it carries.

My humble wish is to offer hope to all the people who are fighting their own battles.

My experiences shared in this book are decades old. The divine experiences shall continue with the next volume.

The Divine Guidance to Write This Book

Once while meditating in 2020, I was guided to write my life story and experiences. Soon after, while meditating, I saw blue water with a ripple, the ripple slowly turned into a chakra and was rotating on a finger. There was blue everywhere, and I could feel some godly presence. Instantly, I saw Lord Krishna sitting next to me. He had brought a book and a pen. The bookmark had a silk tassel, the book had a golden border, and the pen appeared as a brush, an ancient one, like the one we dip in ink and write. Lord Krishna smilingly opened the book; the pages were white and clear. He kept the pen at the binding in the center of the book, told me to write, blessed me, and left.

A few days later, Lord Krishna came again while I was meditating and, smilingly asked me why I hadn't started writing yet. I said, "I will start writing after seeking blessings from my Poojya Guruji."

He said, "Okay, but remember, I will keep coming to you to remind you to write. Also, you will be able to talk to me even when you are not meditating. I will come when you call out to me." He stayed for some time, blessed me, and left.

Once, during evening meditation, while I was breathing through my chakras, I felt a strong pull below the Mooladhara chakra and underneath the meditation mat, on which I was sitting. Fearless, I continued breathing through my chakras. After some seconds the ground below me opened, and I could see darkness. It was inviting. My soul went below the base and I could see a few stages, I counted them (I am not supposed to reveal the count). I didn't enter any of them but came back. Just a few seconds before my meditation was over, I saw and felt Lord Krishna's presence next to me on the right side. He said "Time to meet your Guruji" and disappeared (It was a reminder from Lord Krishna to meet Guruji to seek his blessings for writing the Book, as I was firm on meeting Guruji before I could start it).

After this experience, I messaged Guruji about the insights I received, also about a member of our meditation group (a closed group created by Guruji) encouraging me to note my experiences, saying someday I could publish a book, Guruji replied, "It's correct." Just after receiving Guruji's blessings to write the book, some members of our meditation group wrote to me to write a book on my beautiful experiences. I was happy to receive his blessings by message; however, I wished to meet him in person and seek blessings before I began the work. Due to the nationwide lockdown with the increasing number of COVID-19 patient cases, it was not easy to immediately visit Guruji.

Later in 2020, I met Guruji to seek his blessings to write the book. I had bought a diary with the words written on the book cover, "A journey of a thousand miles begins with a single step." On my visit to Guruji's home, I requested him to sign the diary for me in which I would write about my experiences. He happily said, "Yes", and asked me, "Have you brought the diary?" I answered positively and handed over the diary to him. He read the words on the book cover and said, "It is true." Immense joy could be seen on his face. Before I could give him a pen to sign, he rushed to a room, brought a pen, wrote blessings, signed, and mentioned the date in the diary. He said to me this diary won't be enough. He told me to keep writing to him and share my experiences, saying, "All your experiences are correct."

Acknowledgments

I wish to thank my Guru, all my Gurus, and all my well-wishers.

My Guru your guidance, support, and blessings have been the foundation of my growth and strength. Each step I take reflects your wisdom and encouragement.

I am deeply grateful for your presence in my life and for being a part of my journey. Your love and blessings are the light that inspires me to move forward with gratitude and humility.

My well-wishers, your silent prayers and kindness have uplifted me in ways words cannot express.

Spiritual Practices

Spirituality is a deeply personal and transformative journey beyond religious teachings, rituals, or beliefs. It is the exploration of one's inner self and connection with the greater universe, often leading to profound self-awareness, peace, and a sense of purpose. Spirituality transcends cultural boundaries, offering a universal path for those seeking meaning in life and a connection with Divine, nature, or their highest self. Spirituality and religion are different.

Benefits of Embracing Spirituality

Emotional Resilience: Spirituality provides strength during challenging times, offering hope, comfort, and a framework to cope with suffering.

Enhanced Relationships: By fostering empathy and understanding, spirituality improves interpersonal connections and promotes harmony.

Personal Growth: Spiritual exploration often leads to releasing limiting beliefs, healing past wounds, and accepting growth and transformation.

A Sense of Belonging: Spirituality reduces feelings of isolation and promotes unity, whether through a spiritual community or a connection with nature and the universe.

Meditation: A Pathway to Inner Peace and Self-Discovery

Meditation is a practice of calming the mind, focusing inward, and cultivating awareness to achieve mental clarity and emotional balance. Meditation helps quiet the mind's incessant chatter, allowing individuals to connect with their inner selves and the present moment. Imagination during meditation is not recommended. Only a Guru can tell you whether your experiences are real or unreal. Meditation may not give immediate results, in some cases, it may take many lifetimes, especially Kundalini meditation. Meditation is about awareness, gradually enabling practitioners to tap into their innate wisdom and peace when practised along with a disciplined life and under the supervision of a Guru.

Benefits of Meditation

Meditation is not about escaping reality but engaging with it fully. Over time, it rewires the mind, fostering a calm and compassionate perspective. It bridges the gap between the external and internal worlds, empowering practitioners to face life's challenges gracefully. Meditation is a journey, a practice of returning to the present moment, where true peace resides.

Pranayama: The Art of Breath Control for Mind-Body Harmony

Pranayama: It is a practice of regulating the breath to enhance physical, mental, and spiritual well-being. The breath is a natural, unconscious process that sustains life. However, pranayama teaches us to bring conscious awareness to the breath and control its rhythm and flow. It increases awareness of the present moment and helps one connect to one's inner energy source. By mastering pranayama, individuals can harness the power of the breath to restore balance, boost energy, and cultivate inner peace when practised correctly under the guidance of a Guru

Benefits of Pranayama

Mental Clarity and Focus: Pranayama helps clear the mind, improving concentration and cognitive function. It provides a sense of calm and sharpness, reducing mental clutter and anxiety.

Physical Health: Regular practice enhances lung capacity, improves oxygen circulation, and relaxes the body and mind, promoting better sleep. It also strengthens the respiratory system and helps detoxify the body by expelling toxins through deep breaths.

If not practiced correctly, both pranayama and Meditation can have adverse effects on a practitioner's mental, physical, and emotional well-being. Hence, it is important to seek the guidance and supervision of a Guru for these practices.

Understanding Kundalini Awakening

Kundalini is a Sanskrit word that comes from "Kundal," meaning "a ring," specifically referring to the circular rings worn in the ears. The imagery of a coiled snake with its head resting at the top of the coil symbolizes protection over something hidden. In Vedic philosophy, Kundalini depicts a serpent coiling layer by layer to safeguard something of great significance. This concept embodies a powerful and vital energy that must be approached with respect and awakened with care. Ancient Vedic tales frequently recount stories of snakes guarding a precious gem known as "Mani" or "Naagmani."

In Indian fables, the Nag is often depicted as the guardian of precious gems, symbolizing the Kundalini energy within us. Each person is born with this energy, though it remains dormant until awakened. Kundalini energy lies dormant in the human body, like a sleeping snake. By default, this energy remains unconscious but can be awakened through meditation, yoga, pranayama, kriyas, and other spiritual practices. When awakened, Kundalini is a powerful force that can profoundly transform a person's life. The energy flows upwards from the Mooladhara Chakra to the Ajna Chakra (Third Eye), activating and opening each chakra.

Kundalini represents the feminine divine power that lies dormant at the base of the spine, below the Mooladhara chakra.

Awakening Kundalini energy requires readiness and preparation. Kundalini yoga and meditation are potent practices for this purpose, capable of opening up numerous dimensions in a person's life. However, awakening Kundalini prematurely or without proper guidance can lead to significant negative consequences. It is crucial to engage in these practices under vigilant supervision to avoid adverse effects.

Despite the abundant literature on the subject, attempting these practices solely based on self-study can be perilous. The process involves disciplined steps, focused practice, and significant lifestyle adjustments, all of which should be undertaken with experienced guidance to ensure safety and effectiveness. A person has to be in a pure state of body and mind for Kundalini awakening.

Kundalini Awakenings are the rarest phenomenon, requiring a very informed and disciplined lifestyle to experience. They activate the dormant energies in the body, splurging from the base of the spine to the crown. The experience is said to be parallel to nothing else and truly exceptional.

The Kundalini awakening is the epitome of spiritual consciousness, although it lies dormant in every individual, not everyone can unleash it.

Chakras

A chakra is an energy center in the subtle body that regulates the flow of physical, emotional, and spiritual energy. Originating from Sanskrit, meaning "wheel," chakras are often visualized as spinning vortexes of energy aligned along the spine, each governing specific aspects of life and consciousness.

There are 114 chakras, 112 are inside the body and the other 2 chakras are outside the body. The main chakras are the

Mooladhara, Swadhisthana, Manipura, Anahata, Vishuddhi, Ajna, and Sahasrara.

Chakras include the Lalata chakra, Golata chakra, and Lalana chakra. These chakras can be sensed only after Kundalini awakening.

There are 72000 Nadis or pathways. They channel the life force into the physical body. Sushumna Nadi, Ida, and Pingala are the 3 main Nadis.

When the chakras or Nadis are blocked, it can disrupt the flow of vital energy (often called prana, chi, or life force) throughout the body, mind, and spirit. This imbalance can manifest in various ways, affecting physical health, emotional well-being, and spiritual growth.

A Guru can guide you how to unblock your chakras and Nadis. There are techniques such as pranayama, meditation, yoga etc.

- **Mooladhara Chakra**

  The Mooladhara Chakra, or root chakra, is the first chakra and serves as the foundation of our existence. "Mula" or "Mool" means root, and "Adhara" means basis. This chakra is symbolized by a red lotus with four petals. Located near the dormant Kundalini energy,

  The Mooladhara chakra is the origin of the three main psychic channels or Nadis: Ida, Pingala, and Sushumna. It is the resting place of the dormant serpent and the source of all energies, sexual, emotional, mental, psychic, and spiritual. Increasing your consciousness of this chakra, even outside of meditation, enhances the likelihood of activating it.

  Colour – Red

- **Swadhisthana Chakra**

The Swadhisthana chakra is the storehouse of all our past mental impressions and the most deep-rooted instincts of humankind. By purifying this chakra, we transcend our animal instincts. This chakra is represented as a six-petalled lotus.

The Swadhisthana, or second chakra, is often blocked by fear, particularly the fear of death. Situated two finger-widths above the Mooladhara chakra, the Swadhisthana is the repository of unconscious desires.

The Swadhisthana chakra holds all our past mental impressions and the most deep-rooted instincts of humankind. Purifying this chakra allows us to transcend our basic animal instincts.

Colour – Orange

- **Manipura Chakra**

The Manipura, or Solar Plexus Chakra, is the third primary chakra In line with the navel, towards the spine. Its name translates to "resplendent gem," with "mani" meaning gem. It is represented by a ten-petalled lotus.

Activating the Manipura chakra brings happiness and a strong focus on karma. This chakra helps dispel doubts about destiny, as those who embrace karma understand its role in shaping life. Known as the hidden gem, the Manipura chakra signifies our ability to influence our destiny through our actions.

Colour – Yellow

- **Anahata Chakra**

Anahata, which means "unhurt, unstruck, and unbeaten," refers to a Vedic concept of balance, peace, and serenity.

This chakra is represented as a twelve-petalled lotus with two triangles intersecting inside.

The Anahata, or Heart Chakra, is located in the central channel of the spine near the heart. Its true location is at the center of the chest, the seat of the soul (atman). Serving as the bridge between the lower and upper chakras, the Anahata chakra fosters love, compassion, and devotion. Activating this chakra brings harmonious relationships, forgiveness, trust, and unconditional love, surrounding one with warmth and connection.

Colour – green

- **Vishuddhi Chakra**

Vishuddhi, also known as the throat chakra, is the fifth primary chakra in our body. Positioned at the throat region above the collarbone and at the center of the larynx, it marks the first upper chakra. Vishuddhi governs all energies associated with the throat, particularly those related to vocal expression. When this chakra is in balance, communication skills are significantly enhanced. It is represented as a sixteen-petalled lotus.

Activation of the Vishuddhi chakra transforms a yogi into a capable leader, an eloquent speaker, and a person of great influence.

Colour – Blue

- **Ajna Chakra**

Ajna, also known as the third-eye chakra or Guru Chakra, is the sixth primary chakra in Hindu tradition. Positioned between the eyebrows in the center of the forehead, Ajna serves as the seat of wisdom and intuition. The term "Guru Chakra" stems from its role in providing direction and answers to life's questions.

Through dedicated meditation focused on the third eye, practitioners can attain profound wisdom. However, reaching this chakra requires discipline, as distractions can delay achieving clarity and insight. Once activated, Ajna enhances a person's clarity of vision, and ability to imagine. It is represented as a two-petalled lotus

Ajna is often likened to the eye of wisdom (jnana), or the eye of Shiva. It is considered the final chakra, where inner guidance from our higher selves or inner Gurus is accessed through meditation.

Colour - Indigo

Activating this chakra enhances wisdom and intuition, fostering steadiness, strength, and heightened awareness.

- **Sahasrara Chakra**

Sahasrara, or the Crown Chakra, is widely regarded as the seventh chakra in the human body. It represents the pinnacle of spiritual evolution and consciousness.

Activation of the Crown chakra grants a yogi profound understanding and clarity in life, free from confusion. It symbolizes higher-level awareness, realization, boundless peace, and liberation from limiting patterns. It is represented as a thousand-petalled lotus.

The Crown chakra signifies a state of Shunya (void) or Samadhi (oneness). It connects to the supreme power, offering enduring happiness and freedom—a state achieved only by exceptional spiritual leaders. This chakra transcends sorrow, fear, ignorance, and other human frailties, embodying limitless power and infinity.

Accessing the Sahasrara Chakra is immensely challenging, requiring years of intense spiritual practice, and divine will. It is represented as a thousand-petalled lotus, with each petal symbolizing profound aspects of consciousness. Situated at the crown of my head, the chakra holds the jyotirlinga or lingam of pure light and consciousness.

Bindu Visarga

Bindu Visarga, meaning "Point of Release," is a subtle spiritual center located near the crown of my head, associated with the Sahasrara Chakra. It symbolizes the source of creation and the flow of divine energy or nectar (amrita). In yogic traditions, it is seen as a focal point for higher consciousness and spiritual awakening, linking the individual self to universal consciousness.

Jalneti

Jalneti is a technique traditionally practiced by yogis to maintain health and, crucially, to enhance their breathing for uninterrupted yogic practices. There are Jalneti pots available in the market or online.

To do Jalneti, take lukewarm saline water and fill the Jalneti pot with this saline water up to the brim, one can dip one's finger to check the temperature of the water. Tilt your head, insert the nozzle of the Jalneti pot into one nostril, and allow the water to flow out from the other nostril. Repeat this process with the other nostril as well. One can gargle with the leftover saline water

Self-healing

Self-healing is an act of healing oneself, by placing one hand on our Sahasrara Chakra and the other hand on the part or organ of our body that require healing. Alternatively, we can place both hands on the part or organ that needs healing by saying positive affirmations like "I am feeling better / I am healing, all my diseases are leaving me / God or Guru is healing me, etc." This is effective after one is taught by a Guru.

Role of Food

Food plays an important role in our spiritual progress. One needs to keep one's body always alkaline. One can research on alkaline and acidic foods and decide what is right for one's body. Try to avoid acidic foods. They can cause serious health problems. Also, juices, self-healing, meditation, and exercises help a lot

The Importance of Daily Water Consumption

Water is essential for our body's health and well-being. It supports vital functions such as digestion, nutrient absorption, and toxin removal. Staying hydrated improves energy, focus, and skin health while helping regulate body temperature and maintain overall balance.

Individual water needs vary depending on factors like age, weight, activity level, and climate. While general guidelines suggest drinking enough to stay hydrated, a better approach is to listen to your body. Thirst, dark-coloured urine, or dry skin may indicate the need for more water. One should consume sufficient water.

Incorporate water-rich foods like fruits and vegetables into your diet and keep a water bottle handy. Staying hydrated is a simple yet powerful habit for a vibrant and healthy life.

My Formative Years

I was named Shashtria by my parents. I could speak a few languages while growing up. As a child, my hobbies were solving puzzles, reading books, painting, playing all sorts of games, and collecting old notes, coins of different countries, stamps, rare stones, and leaves. I was very active and good at observing things, and learning came to me easily. I was always a cheerful and happy-go-lucky child. All the children who came across me liked my presence and association. At a very young age, I could sense energies. Whatever I said or predicted would come true. I could foresee things well in advance.

I remember my grandmother and how she adored me and also worshipped me at times. Granny was the only person who pampered me. After Granny, almost everyone who appeared on my journey intended to destroy my light and suppress my spirit.

However, equally true and more relevant is the fact that at every step where I was nearing irreversible damage, there was a divine presence to gently guide me to safety, to whom I will be eternally grateful.

All my dreams were blessings. I still remember, as a child, things were shown to me in advance, and I used to tell my mother, father, and grandma. They listened to me very carefully, as whatever I predicted always came true.

At the age of 10, due to an untoward incident that took place in the church, I stopped believing in God and refused to go to church with my family. I had many unanswered questions. Many years later, my friend insisted that I visit churches and temples, and again, I began to visit holy places.

Seva at Gurudwara

An incident I remember from my school days is how my friends and I would walk home together, passing a Gurudwara along the way.

One day, I decided to go inside, as, for quite some time, some unseen divine force would try to draw me inside the Gurudwara. I could sense it. Once the gate was slightly opened, no one was at the entrance. I asked my friends if they would join me, and they all agreed. We silently entered. A few people were cleaning and arranging things. While passing, to my left, I saw a guava tree. It was small in height but had a lot of fruits on it. We had never seen a fruit-laden guava tree before, all of us were admiring the tree, wondering how such a small tree could bear so many fruits. One friend who was a little taller than us thought of plucking some guavas. I told her not to. "It is not correct. Let's go home." Just then from nowhere, a tall man with a long beard, blue turban, and navy-blue clothing came in front of us. He directly asked me, "Do you want guavas?" I didn't answer. He said, "Your friends want some." I said, "Yes." We all were scared as we had entered without permission, and didn't know the way out. He began to pluck some guavas. He gave my friends, and lastly gave me one too, saying, "We generally don't allow people to pass through, but you and your friends can pass from here daily. Also, you can pluck guavas, but don't pluck every day, or else the fruits will get over. Let them grow well, then pluck." I thanked him. He then guided us to the way out. The gate was kept open from the next day onwards, and the chain was removed. We passed through the way daily, joining hands. One day, I went and sat inside the prayer hall. After a few days, I began doing selfless service, such as sweeping the floor, dusting, and watering the plants. We sometimes had extra classes. The people of the Gurudwara would wait for me. I felt safe and was loved by all.

As I grew older, I helped serve langar (food for everyone) and cleaned and dusted the devotees' footwear. The main priest would bless me and let me hold the Guru Granth Sahib for a few minutes before placing it back under the canopy. I learned the Ardas (prayer) and many hymns.

My mother and father used to scold me for coming home late. They found out later what I was doing all this time while coming home late. There was a Guru Nanak Jayanti function, and I was chosen to recite the Ardas on stage. My parents were surprised that I had even learned some Punjabi. I then asked my parents to hire a teacher to teach me Punjabi, which they did.

There is unexplained happiness in serving, being kind, and giving pure love and compassion to everyone without expecting anything in return.

Lord Ayyappa Procession

My parents got my ears pierced when I was a baby, but they closed as I refused to wear earrings. I would tell them, "When the time comes, I will pierce my ears and would wear earrings on my own."

As a child, I once insisted on taking part in a procession of Lord Ayyappa where young girls carry lamps in their hands. In this procession, strictly Brahmin girls below 10 years of age participated. Knowing I would not give up, my father requested the chairman of the committee who organized the yearly event to allow me to participate. The chairman said, "It is only for Brahmins." Somehow, after looking at me, he agreed and told my father, "She will have to wear earrings, and she should be dressed in South Indian traditional clothing like the other girls."

I happily agreed to get my ears pierced once again, and Granny, while combing my hair, asked me, "Has the time come to wear earnings?" I happily replied, "Yes Granny." Though my parents were not happy, looking at my happiness, they bought me the traditional clothes and the jewellery required and even got my ears pierced. Though it was painful, I wore the earrings with a smile. I took part in the procession, and everything went smoothly. I still remember seeing Lord Ayyappa's shining, lively eyes looking at me when I went to seek his blessings. I felt he was really in front of me, and I told my father the same. My father and his relatives told me, "You are lucky. Bow your head and seek his blessings."

The Lepers

People are afraid of lepers, but I'm not. When I was growing up, after Sunday mass and on feast days, I would ask my father to buy bread and sometimes milk for them. My father would tell me to give it to them from a distance and not to touch them because leprosy is contagious.

Once, in my excitement to help, I accidentally touched a leper's hand full of sores and pus. My father threw everything away, scolded me, and made me wash my hands many times. He and my mother watched me for a few months to see if I got infected, checking my hands daily. They were relieved once they realised I was fine but warned me not to do it again. I promised to be careful and requested my parents to allow me to give them bread. After that, I was more cautious, knowing that if I made another mistake, they wouldn't buy bread for the lepers again.

Many years later, I regularly visited an elderly aunty leper at the vegetable market. She had a usual spot and would always tell me she felt loved and thanked me, asking if I could visit her every day. I explained that I couldn't come daily because my house was far away, but I promised to visit once a week. Whenever she saw me from a distance, she would start smiling. There was also an elderly uncle near my house, outside a bank, who would smile whenever he saw me. Both were lepers, I used to buy them whatever they asked for and give them some money. Their happiness made me happy too.

Thaipusam Festival Procession

Thaipusam is a festival celebrated by the Tamil Hindu community on the full moon in the Tamil month of Thai (January/February). It commemorates the occasion when Goddess Parvati gave Lord Murugan (Kartikeya) a Vel (spear) to vanquish the demon Surapadman and his brothers. It is also believed to mark Lord Murugan's birthday.

On one Thaipusam day, I felt restless at home and insisted that my father take me outside, sensing a procession was near. He agreed, and we stepped out to find a crowd had already gathered, with the sounds of drums and other instruments filling the air.

The Thaipusam procession was passing through our locality, creating a celebratory atmosphere. Devotees in the procession were in a trance-like state, with some having body piercings, others carrying pots of water, and many playing musical instruments. At the end of the procession was a chariot with a golden idol of Lord Murugan, adorned with colourful flowers and surrounded by offerings of fruits.

As the procession reached us, I let go of my father's hand and joined in. I instinctively took a place at the front of the procession, as if some divine energy had asked me to do this. I was in a trance, and I realised people were approaching me, washing my feet, and offering flowers. The procession paused for a while as the crowd continued with the holy rituals. Eventually, I continued walking with the procession until my father pulled me out at the end.

Life-Altering Moments in My Youth

I lost my father early in life. Mine was not a smooth life, but I was sheltered, fed well, and looked after.

In my 10th grade, an incident shook me to the core. It changed my life forever. I lost my life and got it back. I was brought back to life by Divine. I still remember everything.

Once I was on my way to teaching some students. I was lost in thought because my brother had fought with me before I left. I crossed one side of the main road and was in the middle of crossing to the other side when I just froze, stuck in heavy traffic. A large bus was about to run over me. People on the other side were in a panic, thinking I would die. Suddenly, a man appeared out of nowhere and rescued me.

The traffic slowed as he gently held my hand, and helped me cross the road safely, and then he disappeared. I felt the hand of Lord Jesus. This incident is very close to my heart. I could feel his purity. This occurred on a road, where many accidents happen daily.

Leaving Home in Pain

I was a very healthy kid since childhood, but at the age of 16, my life took an unexpected turn. One day, I developed a fever and vomited, prompting a visit to our family doctor.

He conducted tests and referred me to a top hospital, where further examinations revealed an alarming diagnosis, and immediate surgery was deemed necessary to save my life.

Although I had doubts about the situation, my mother decided to proceed with the surgery, supported by a generous benefactor who covered the costs. At the hospital, I encountered a series of unsettling events, including being registered under a false age and false name and vague explanations from the medical staff. During surgery, I regained consciousness before the anesthesia fully wore off, forcing the doctors to hastily complete the procedure. They informed my mother that the surgery was incomplete and that further interventions might be needed later.

Post-surgery recovery was painful, both physically and emotionally. Amid the challenges, a kind, unknown doctor encouraged me to stand and walk again. His compassionate presence gave me strength, but when I tried to thank him later, I discovered that no one at the hospital knew of him. The staff told me as per your and your mother's description, there is no such doctor who visits the hospital. This led me and my mother to believe he was a divine visitor who appeared to help me during my darkest moments.

Returning home, I faced unexpected hostility from my family. My brother and mother isolated me and made it clear I was no longer welcome in the house. Unable to bear the emotional and physical strain, I was forced to leave my home and start a new chapter in my life.

Post this, I couldn't study further because of serious health issues. My health deteriorated and from then on, my life was in and out of hospitals.

Over the next years, the range of people who came in my path as challenges extended to immediate family, friends, doctors, and others.

Although the journey was filled with pain and uncertainty, I found the courage to move forward, drawing strength from the kindness of strangers and my inner resilience.

Starting a New Life

A divine soul offered to help me and took care of me in my difficult times. I was told, "Never feel that you are alone. You will never feel there's no one for you. I will take care of you as parents take care of their children. Don't think of your mother and brother. They will pay for what they have done to you. They will soon lose everything, and they will come back to you. Be careful, they will try to take away whatever you have. I will always be there with you, even if I leave this world, I will always be there with you."

Those words were the only assurance I had. I had lost everything in life. Because of Divine Soul's goodwill, I was not on the streets but had a shelter to live in.

My mother's place was 15-20 minutes away, but she never tried to look for me or know what condition I was in.

Moving out of my parents' house changed a lot of things. I became independent, completed my education, and worked my way to survive without deviating from the right path.

I began by teaching nursery kids, then moved on to teaching school students, and eventually became a full-time tutor, working from early morning until 10 p.m. with just a one-hour lunch break. My best memories are from the time I spent with the kids. During this period, I managed to work and study simultaneously. I was married briefly.

After a few decades, my mother and brother realised their mistakes and asked for forgiveness. Instantly, I forgave them.

Visions and Divine Encounters

Although my life was full of struggles, I experienced a beautiful phase where I had visions of Gods & Goddesses who reminded me to visit their temples. There was some divine power watching over me always. From an early age, I used to get visions of Lord Jesus, Mother Mary, many Saints, Gods, Goddesses, Archangels, Lord Ganesh, Lord Shiva sitting with his eyes closed, and even Lord Nataraja. When asked, I used to describe everything in detail.

I had divine experiences of closed temple and church doors being opened for me, as I was welcomed by the main priests. The temples were of Lord Ganesh in Ganpatipule, Goddess Vani in Nashik, and Goddess Mayakka in Belgaum, Karnataka. At the temples of the Goddesses mentioned above, I was called ahead by the priests, and one of them smeared my forehead completely with bhandara (a yellow turmeric powder).

At Ekvira in Lonavala, we reached late and the temple was locked. Seeing me, the priests opened the temple gate, and I could have a soulful darshan.

It continued with Goddesses Jivdani, Renuka Devi, and many more. I visited these places after having visions during my teens.

I have had many divine experiences in Shirdi. I used to have visions, and mantras were shown to me. I would be shown how and when to recite them. I still remember them.

Once during my difficult times, towards the end of my meditation, I saw Tipu Sultan blessing me with the courage to keep going. I was guided that everything that we read is not true. A lot of things were revealed.

More than 30 years ago, I visited the shrine of Infant Jesus in Nasik after a vision. By the time I reached there, it was afternoon. The church was closed. On enquiring when the church would open, the security guard at the gate replied, "In the evening." I thought, "Since it will open in the evening, it will be better, to go back to Mumbai and come some other day." I had planned to visit the church and leave for Mumbai immediately. Just then, the guard opened the gate and told me, to come inside. He walked with me, opened the church door, and allowed me to go in. I entered the church, sat down, and offered my gratitude to Infant Jesus for everything. Looking at the statue, I could see baby Jesus lively, smiling at me. For a while, I was amazed by the grace I received. Soon, I left thanking the guard. The same thing occurred at The Mount Mary church and the Vailankanni church in Mumbai.

Maa Jivdani

In 2005, I met a girl who was my doctor's assistant. During my regular BP checkups, she would always move my appointment ahead of all the other patients as soon as she saw me walk in. If anyone questioned her, she would say that I had come earlier, given my name, and then left for some work. This occurred every time I visited the clinic. I would get my BP checked, thank her, and leave.

One day, she called me and said, "Ma'am, I've noticed that I get good vibes whenever you come to the clinic. My day goes well. The doctor also says there's an energy change whenever you visit the clinic. He says you're a good person. I wish you could come to the clinic daily, but that would be selfish of me. I hope you get well soon with your BP issues forever."

I thanked her for her kind words and asked her, "Why do you lie to the other patients about my appointment?"

She replied, "I don't know the reason, but felt that you shouldn't have to wait."

Soon, she began calling me every day, and we became good friends over time. One day, I shared with her my experiences of having visions and flashes of the Jivdani Goddess and the temple.

I asked her if she had ever been to the Jivdani temple. She replied, "Yes, a long time ago."

Then she asked if I had been there. I said, "No."

She then told me, "Maa is calling you. Please visit the temple whenever possible." I said, "I can't promise, but if the Goddess wishes, I will visit her."

Strangely, the next morning, I found a picture of the Goddess in a small glass frame on top of my fridge. I took it in my hands, wondering where it had come from. I clicked a picture and showed it to my friend, telling her how miraculously the picture of the Goddess had appeared in my home. She immediately recognized it and said it was Maa Jivdani. Amazed by this, I took it as a clear indication to visit the Goddess.

I requested my close friend to join me, and after a few days, we went to the Jivdani temple. There were many stalls at the base of the hill, selling holy articles. I saw photos of the

Goddess, which looked similar to the one that had mysteriously appeared on top of my fridge.

The temple is situated on a hill and requires a climb of more than a thousand steps to reach. By the time we climbed our way to the temple, it was afternoon, and the darshan was paused. Inside the temple, the hall was packed with people waiting to receive the Goddess's blessings.

My friend and I noticed a person arranging steel barricades to manage the crowd. We asked him when the darshan would resume, and he said it would be in the evening. We thanked him and sat down to wait for our turn. As he finished arranging the barricades, he went into the inner sanctum to clear the offerings placed at the feet of the Goddess. We could see both him and the Goddess.

Within a minute, he abruptly stopped what he was doing, turned around, and began removing the barricades. The entire crowd, including us, was overjoyed. He unlocked the second-to-last barricade, cleared the way, and signalled for me to come forward.

I looked at him, unsure if he was really calling me. He loudly called out in Marathi, "You come. The rest, sit down."

I got up and requested him to allow my friend to join me. He agreed, saying, "Okay, but you go in first." I signalled to my friend and proceeded straight to the inner sanctum.

Inside, two priests approached and blessed me by placing their hands on my head together. One of them touched the idol and applied a tilak (a vertical line) on my forehead with the red vermillion from the Goddess's idol. They gave me jaggery and poha to eat. When I tried to share it with my friend, they insisted that I eat it alone. They gave my friend some prasad and handed me a bag containing leaves, flowers, coconuts, and coconut sweets. I bowed my head, thanked the Goddess for her kindness and blessings, and stood in front of her for a while.

I told the priests about the events that led me there. They both said, "Maa wanted you to visit her. You are blessed." After blessing me, the priests left the sanctum and told me to come whenever I wished.

Before leaving, we thanked the person who had let us in. He humbly said, "I didn't do anything. Maa had called you." He joined his hands, looking at me, and I joined my hands in gratitude, feeling blessed and happy. My friend was overjoyed and thanked me, having witnessed similar incidents with me at many holy places before.

We went to the upper level, as guided, and found a statue of Goddess Maa Kali. I placed a coin on the stone, and it stuck. I repeated this without praying for anything, and each time, the coin stuck. I managed to stick 21 coins in total. This phenomenon has occurred at a few temples I've visited. People gathered around to see how my coins stuck while theirs kept falling into the donation box.

After seeking Maa Kali's blessings, we left. Later, I visited this temple a few more times when guided. Each visit was more beautiful and profound than the last.

Siddhivinayak Temple

I used to visit the Siddhivinayak temple every Tuesday, sit on the steps inside the temple, in front of Lord Ganesh's idol, look at him for a few minutes, and leave. I never asked for any favour or blessings. It was as if Bappa wanted me to visit him, and I would be there.

Inside the inner sanctum, though I would stand to the extreme left or right, trying to avoid people, somehow the crowd would push me, and I would always end up right in front of Lord Ganesh's idol. After reaching there, no one would push me. I would get a minute or two to be in front of Siddhivinayak, which is a rare fortune. The main priest in the gabhara (inner sanctum) one day spoke to me in Marathi, "Come, Bappa is calling you. I have noticed you always reach in front of Ganpati Bappa on your own. It is his wish. For many years, I have seen you coming. Our eyes are everywhere; nothing is missed, and you're a blessed one to reach him without any effort."

The priest or the security normally don't let anyone wait for more than a few seconds. However, I was never told to move. My maid and friends had noticed this. The security in charge, who handled the crowd, would tell them to leave and allow me to stay.

The priest used to give me rare flowers, coconuts, modaks, and flowers, and once even a gold coin with Lord Ganesh's imprint, and many more things. The priests would always remove a garland offered to the idol and say, "Take this." Once, I was given a garland of 11 coconuts which was difficult to carry. He put it in a tray and told me, "Take this, use it in your daily cooking. Do not give it to anyone. I have made this for you after having a vision." He was the same priest who would be there every Tuesday for many years.

Since childhood, I have had unforgettable memories and witnessed miracles during the Ganesh festival and while visiting Lord Ganesh's temples and other temples.

Bhagwan Nityanand

One day, I had a vision of Vajreshwari and the surrounding Ganeshpuri. A temple with the same name appeared to me, and I saw some steps leading up to it. I had no idea where this place was or how to get there. I called my friend from a PCO

(Public Call Offices in the earlier days of Mumbai were lifelines of communication, bustling hubs where people queued to make affordable calls across the city and beyond) and asked if she could accompany me. She immediately agreed, and we set off.

She is the same friend who has travelled with me to many of the holy places I've visited. She is older than me, so I felt safe going out with her. Although she is not religious, she always loved to accompany me whenever I had a vision.

Her mother was very fond of me and used to tell me, "Never think you are alone. We are with you." She encouraged me to visit the places I saw in my visions, saying, "God wants you to do it. You must do it, and my daughter will accompany you." My friend's elder brother was also very supportive.

Every place of worship I visited was shown to me in a vision, and we always reached them easily. Often, we weren't charged any money by bus conductors, they would give us tickets and walk away without taking any payment. Sometimes, I even received extra money back at railway ticket counters. When I tried to return the extra money, they would refuse to take it and offer confusing explanations. This occurred wherever I went.

For Vajreshwari, we decided to travel by train and headed to the railway station ticket booking counter. There, we asked the ticket issuer for guidance on how to reach Vajreshwari. He gave us our tickets, some extra money, and clear directions. We reached Virar and went to the auto stand as instructed. I asked an auto driver if he could take us to Vajreshwari.

He inquired, "Where do you want to go, Ganeshpuri or Vajreshwari?"

I replied, "Vajreshwari."

He pointed to a line of autos and told us to go there to find one for Vajreshwari.

We approached the first auto in the line and asked the driver if he could take us to Vajreshwari. He was wiping the front glass and said, "Yes," without looking at us. He was dressed entirely in white, wearing a white cloth cap and even white footwear. We both got into the rickshaw and just then, a couple approached. The girl asked me if the auto was going to Vajreshwari, and I said yes. It was a shared auto, so they joined us.

The girl sat in the back with us, and the guy sat in the front seat, with the driver. We asked the driver how much he would charge, and he said 200 rupees. The boy asked if it was 50 rupees per person, but the driver just nodded and started driving. After a few minutes, he slowed down and asked me again, "Ganeshpuri or Vajreshwari?"

He said, "You can go to Ganeshpuri, where there is a Samadhi Mandir of Bhagwan Nityananda. People from all over the world come there for his darshan." Hearing this, the couple jumped out of the auto, saying they didn't want to go to Ganeshpuri. I told the driver that we didn't know anything about him but that he could take us there. He happily drove off at full speed, singing a bhajan.

After a while, he dropped us near a small shop, amidst greenery, and said, "Go from here, and you will find the Samadhi temple."

I gave him a 100-rupee note, but he said it was 60 rupees. I reminded him that he had said 50 rupees each, totalling 100 rupees. I said I didn't have any change. My friend didn't have change either, so I told him to keep the extra. He refused. I then asked him to wait while I got change from the shop. Throughout the journey, he had hidden his face and never looked at us.

I rushed to the shop, where a friendly aunty was managing it. She happily gave me the change. Filled with happiness, I ran a few steps to give him the money, but as he saw me coming, he sped off. I ran after his auto, calling out and reminding him that he hadn't taken the money, but he didn't stop.

I went back to the shop and asked the aunty if she knew him. She said she had seen him for the first time and that no auto driver there wears a white cloth cap. She also mentioned that the rickshaw wasn't from their area. Then, she guided us to the Nityananda Samadhi temple.

When we arrived, the temple was closed for the afternoon. It was an old, large house. The window with iron bars was open, so I peeped inside and saw a statue of a person sitting and some framed photos of saints on the walls. A few people were waiting for darshan as well. Since the Samadhi Mandir was closed, we decided to leave. Just then, a thin man with a dark complexion, short hair, a white thread across his chest, and a white lungi approached us.

He asked me, "Have you come for darshan?"

I said, "Yes."

He had a key on a string tucked to his waist and used it to open an old iron lock. He told me to go in. I told my friend, but she said she wasn't interested and would wait outside. The other people waiting also asked him to let them in, but he didn't reply.

I went in alone, walked around, and sat down, looking at the pictures of all the saints. The man came in and told me this was Bhagwan Nityananda's Samadhi, and that I could seek blessings if I wished. I got up, touched the Samadhi, and came out. He then locked the door, and before we realised it, he had vanished. We looked around to thank him, but he was nowhere to be seen.

On our way back to the road, we met two foreigners, who were looking for the Bhagwan Nityananda Samadhi temple.

They asked for directions, and I told them the temple was closed but that I had somehow managed to see it.

One of them took out a book from her cloth bag and showed me some pictures of Bhagwan Nityananda from his early days and later years. I recognized him immediately as the man who had opened the Samadhi Mandir for me. My friend, seeing the picture, got very excited and told them we had just met him a few minutes ago.

We soon realised that he was also the same person who had driven us there in the auto, the driver who kept hiding his face. The foreigners were amazed and did pranam to me, asking for my phone number. I told them I didn't have one, and when they asked for my address, I politely refused.

As we talked, it started drizzling. We went back to the shop and told the aunty what had happened. She smiled and said, "You were called here. See, it's raining in April. It's a good sign. It hasn't rained properly for two years, and the wells have dried up. I hope it rains this year." I reassured her, saying it would rain and that this was just the beginning.

We happily took an auto to Vajreshwari. When we arrived, we saw people rejoicing because of the rain. We went up to the temple, received blessings, and then left for home. Later, during meditation, I received Bhagwan Nityananda's blessings and realised he was a Siddha Guru. I've had many such experiences throughout my life, starting from when I was a kid.

Shani Shingnapur

There is a beautiful experience that took place many years back. A friend and I had gone to Shirdi. After darshan, we decided to take a stroll towards the main road. On reaching the main road we saw local drivers calling out to people who wanted to travel to Shani Shingnapur. We were standing and watching vehicles getting occupied fast, they were leaving for Shani Shingnapur. A driver requested us a couple of times to seek darshan. Though he was getting passengers, he had kept two seats in the jeep for us. We hadn't been there before and knew nothing about Lord Shani. Since he kept requesting, we decided to go.

It was April, and it began to drizzle. Rain or drizzle in any season has always been a part of my life. It happens when I visit temples, when new places are shown to me in a vision, and on important occasions. A few people close to me are aware of it.

On the way to Shani Shingnapur there were sugarcane carts carrying sugarcane. I was happy seeing the greenery all around. At that time, I used to only drink plain sugarcane juice without ice, masala, or lemon. I felt like tasting a piece of sugarcane, just to check its sweetness, whether it's the same as the ones we get in Mumbai. I requested our driver to drive a little slower, saying I wanted to buy sugarcane.

The driver said, "The person won't give you. The sugarcanes are tied tightly and are going to the sugar factory. He won't be able to remove even one piece from the bundle." I told him, "Let me try requesting."

We were at a railway crossing and had to wait for the train to pass. One sugarcane cart came and halted next to our jeep. As I was thinking about whether to request for sugarcane, the person from the cart got down, pulled out a full sugarcane, smiled at me, gave it to me, and sat back in his cart.

I first wondered how he knew I wanted a sugarcane. Everyone around was in awe too and I was overjoyed and thanked him and offered to pay for it. He politely said no. My friend and others asked for some and even offered to buy.

But, he said, "I can't give."

As soon as I got the sugarcane, the train passed by, and the traffic eased out.

My friend said, "You wished for it, you got it."

I then asked the driver to quickly distribute the sugarcane with everyone in the jeep and to have a piece too. Surprisingly everyone got a decent piece of sugarcane. It didn't fall short. I took a very small piece. All of us were happy and we continued our journey.

When we reached the temple, the streets and temple were decorated as there was some occasion. I was hesitant to enter as we had to leave our footwear outside on the road. In Shirdi, my footwear would regularly get robbed or misplaced and I wouldn't get it back. Since it kept happening, I would leave my footwear in the hotel, and go barefoot for darshan.

Here there was no one to take care of the footwear. I told my friend, "What if they get robbed, I will have to manage with kolhapuris, the only type of footwear available there. I was wary of them as they used to give shoe bites."

Just then an old man dressed in complete white, a cotton kurta, dhoti, and a cloth turban on his head spoke from behind. He said, "Here, no one will rob your footwear. If anyone robs it, he will become mad and roam in this village or he will die. If anyone robs here, he is punished instantly."

I was taken aback by his words and looked at him and it began to rain. He said, "Come with me, I will take you to the temple."

Protecting us from the crowd, he took us inside the temple to a place and told us, "You see the black stone?" We said, "Yes." He continued, "He is Shani Dev. Bow your head and take his blessings."

The place was overcrowded, and people were pushing each other. I had a thought, "How to bow? What if someone pushes me?"

The old man read my mind and said, "No one will touch you. I am here." I bowed my head. Truly no one touched us. He then safely brought us out.

When we came out, my footwear was exactly where I had left it. I thanked him. With a smile on his face, he asked me, "Are you happy that your shoes are safe?"

I said, "Yes. Thank you." He continued, "I have done my duty."

Just then we noticed my friend's footwear was misplaced. We both began looking for it and found it in a few minutes. Till then the old man had disappeared. We looked out for him but couldn't see him.

Direct Darshan

More than 15 years ago, during a crowded day in Shirdi, I was pondering where to leave my footwear near the temple. Suddenly, a man emerged from a side door and instructed me to enter the temple immediately for darshan, granting me exclusive access.

Inside, I found myself standing directly in front of Sri Saibaba's statue. After taking darshan, I turned to thank the man, but he had vanished. No one else seemed to know who he was, and I learned that no one typically enters from that door for darshan. This experience remains etched in my memory, bringing me lasting happiness and contentment.

The Man Who Asked for Rains

Throughout my life, whenever I visited Shirdi, I always travelled by bus with my maid or friends. The last time I visited was when my mother expressed her wish to see the temple. Everyone who had travelled with me before to Shirdi, told my mother, how I always received preferential treatment every time, allowing me to go right to the front of the queue near Sai Baba's idol, while they had to wait in the common line. She was curious to know why I was treated specially at the Saibaba temple.

My mother, myself, and a few people known to us decided to go to Shirdi, and a family friend drove us. As we arrived in Shirdi, an unknown person approached the car and began running alongside it, until we reached our hotel. When we got out, he said, "Tai, mi tumchi vat pahat hota. Mi tumhala sarv jagah dakhvin. Mala paise nako." (Sister, I was waiting for you. I will show you all the places around here, and I don't want any money).

We quickly got ready and headed to the temple, not expecting him, but he was waiting for us and guided us through a special gate. We received a quick darshan without giving any money. My mother was amused when the guard asked me to step in and go to the front through the middle path, right in front of Saibaba. I asked if my mother could join me, but he said she could continue with the others and assured me she wouldn't get lost, and then closed the gate.

The next morning, this man returned to us, looking very sad. He told me that there had been no rain in his village for several years, that the wells had dried up, the land had become barren, and the cattle had been sold off due to water scarcity. He first requested and then pleaded with me to visit his village, expressing his belief that my visit might bring rain.

I hesitated, but eventually agreed, moved by this man's earnest pleas.

The man rode a bicycle, and we followed him in our car. Along the way, he stopped at a temple and requested that we come out of the car. We all exited the car, and he went ahead to buy an aarti thali, then told me, "Tai, come, it is a Panchmukhi Ganpati Mandir."

Everyone entered the temple, but I stood outside, having never heard of a five-faced Lord Ganesh. The priest called me in, and the man handed me the thali. The priest led me to the deity and performed the aarti with the items in the thali. It was a five-faced, black idol of Lord Ganesh.

The priest applied a large tilak on my forehead and said, "Dhanya, Dhanya, Dhanya, if you happen to come by, please visit again." (Dhanya is the Hindi word for "blessed")

Everyone around me watched as I was the only one allowed to touch the deity. The priest informed the others that it was time to close the temple for the afternoon and invited them to come back another time. No money was asked from us. We then continued our journey to the man's village.

On the way, he stopped to buy milk. When we reached his home, he joyfully called out to his wife, saying, "See who has come!" she came out, welcomed us, and invited us inside the house.

He introduced me as "Tai." (sister) He had been talking about. His wife mentioned that he had eagerly been waiting for my visit. I was surprised at this gesture.

He asked his wife to make tea, but I declined, saying, "I don't drink tea," she made tea for my mother and offered me some onions and garlic as a token of gratitude for visiting their home. They were poor but had large hearts. I politely declined and thanked them for their hospitality.

I played with a baby goat and spent some time with them. He showed us his barren land, and I assured him that it would rain this year and things would change. When we were leaving,

I tried to give him some money, but both he and his wife refused, expressing their gratitude for my visit instead. He then asked for my number, promising to call when it rained.

The next morning, as we were preparing to leave for Mumbai, he came again and suggested a shortcut through his village to reach the highway. We left in the evening, and as we neared his village, the weather changed—it became dark and cloudy and started drizzling.

Just as I was about to call him, I saw his call coming in. I told him we were about to reach his place, and that it was drizzling. He was overjoyed and said, "Yes, Tai, I was calling to say the same." He met us with immense joy, pointing out the large raindrops, and said, "I am now sure that it will rain this time." He then followed our vehicle for quite some distance.

On our way back, there were no signboards, as work was going on the highway. We asked few people for directions and followed the road they suggested. After a few minutes of driving, I realised we were in the middle of a jungle. Suddenly, the tyre of our vehicle got punctured, and I could sense there was a crematorium nearby and it was a trap by the negative forces. All the while, I was telling everyone not to take this route, but they paid no heed.

At that moment, a light could be seen. Somehow, we managed to reach to that light. There was a tyre shop in the middle of the jungle. The mechanic got the puncture fixed and told us to go back the same way we had come. The driver suggested going ahead, instead of going back. We kept going ahead for hours, lost in the jungle with no direction. It was a full moon night, I happened to see the moon, and with the moonlight, a crematorium could be seen. Then everyone was scared and began to pray in their own way. At that moment, they could relate to what I was saying.

Suddenly, some words came to my mouth, it went like this (in Sanskrit):

OM Bhur Bhuva Swaha

Tat Savitur Varenayam

Bhargo Devasya Dhimahi

Dhiyo Yoh Nah Prachodayat

I had never heard or read these words before. I came to know through the people who were traveling with me that it is called the Gayatri Mantra. All of us chanted the same Mantra, and within a few minutes, we were on the highway.

A month later, during the rainy season, it rained heavily for three days. The man called me every day to tell me about the rain, repeatedly attributing it to my visit. He urged me to visit their village again if I ever had the chance. He continued to keep in touch for two years. By then, the man had started his theatre. He had become successful and had shows in Mumbai as well.

He sent me an invitation to a show in Mumbai, Thane, and I checked the news-papers to confirm if the show was genuine and found that it was true. His name was listed.

I remember his last call, where he expressed his gratitude once again.

The Guard at Shirdi

Almost 16 years ago, my maid and I went to Shirdi. When we reached for darshan, the line was too long, so we decided to come back later. As we put on our footwear near the Samadhi Mandir, a guard opened the temple door and invited me inside for darshan. I was surprised and hesitant, but he assured me I would be right in front of Sai Baba. Despite requests from others, he only allowed my maid and me to enter, saying Baba had called us.

Once inside, we were indeed right in front of Sai Baba. We were fortunate to witness the Abhishek Pooja, where Sai Baba was bathed in milk, and his clothes were changed. We received prasad, and the priest gave me items offered to Sai Baba: rose flowers, a huge garland, silk cloth from his head, cloth from his shoulders, and holy ash. I bowed to Sai Baba and thanked him.

After the darshan, we went back to thank the guard, but he was gone, and the door was shut. We never saw him again, despite visiting Shirdi almost every month.

Baba's Samadhi

I have many times received huge garlands, fruits, shawls, blessed udi or ash, calendars, and pooja articles at the Shirdi Temple. Countless times, when I reached the Samadhi, the line would be stopped, allowing me to have a peaceful darshan. The guards or constables never hurried or pushed me to finish. I never wasted time, and often, the glass barrier would be removed and I could touch the Samadhi and bow my head to the padukas. Once I finished, the glass would be put back in place.

The Shirdi Procession

Every Thursday night in Shirdi, there is a procession featuring the chanting of hymns and bhajans dedicated to Sai Baba. During this procession, Sai Baba's holy sandals and articles he used are carried in a palanquin. My maid and I went to see the procession, and when the palki came near me, it stopped for a few seconds. I had the opportunity to touch the holy padukas and a few sacred articles. As soon as I took darshan, the palki immediately moved again. I clicked a few pictures, which I still have.

Healings Before Meeting My Guru

As a kid, I wouldn't play with toys and would ask my aunt every time she visited us to get me a toy doctor set. I would request her to get better sets with medicine boxes and instruments. She once asked me the reason as to why I preferred only the doctor set.

I still remember replying to her, "To make the sick alright."

I would feel hurt to see others suffering and I wished to help people.

Years later, while meditating, a voice could be heard saying, "You were born to be a healer. You have healed many unknowingly. You are destined to meet an enlightened master to teach you the perfect way of healing."

There are many instances of me unknowingly healing people before my initiation into Kundalini Meditation or meeting Guruji. Every incident was shown to me in meditation.

Healing My Mother

My mother came to me in a very bad state. She developed pneumonia, then TB (tuberculosis). Her lungs had almost collapsed and were filled with pus. My near ones informed me and witnessed that my mother came to me for help in a dying state.

I took utmost care of her and nursed her to good health. Within a month, she recovered and went home without medication.

After a few years, when my mother came to stay with me permanently, she had health complications and was on medication for 25 years. Her diabetes was (400+), cholesterol (500+), high blood pressure 180/100. Doctors told me she may have an attack anytime. I exhausted my savings for her treatment. At that time, I was getting better at health. I started giving her healing, and within a year, she was free from all the health problems. She would get her regular check-ups done and was very happy to see the positive results. She stopped going to the doctor and stopped taking medicines too.

Healing My Brother

I had healed my brother too, of the 3rd stage of TB, the way I did for my mom. His lungs too had almost collapsed and were filled with pus. He had to undergo minor surgery to drain the pus accumulated in one of his lungs. The doctors said he was still in a critical condition. After a few days of surgery, I told my mother to request the doctor to discharge him. The hospital vibes weren't good. She listened to me. The cause of his contracting TB was the excessive intake of the wrong foods and ice cream from morning to night. He recovered soon with good care.

Another time, my brother called me to say he was not keeping well and had visited the loo almost 14 times that day. He was feeling very weak and was unable to eat or drink anything. I told him his food habits were wrong and not to worry, as he would feel better. I advised him to avoid eating the wrong food.

The next morning, he called to say, "After talking to you the day before, I immediately felt better, my motions stopped, and I felt energetic." He asked me whether I had sent him healing. He continued, "I know you did something, as I realised whenever I fall sick and call you, after some time, I feel ok. You have some powers, but you don't want to tell me." I kept silent.

The Doctor Who Consulted Me

Way back in my teens, I met a doctor who later on went to become my close friend.

I used to visit her clinic to get my BP checked regularly and keep a record, as advised by the surgeon after a major surgery. The doctor would like to spend time with me and requested me to come to her clinic every day, whenever I was free. If I missed going to meet her, she would send someone or ask her mother to call me. Her clinic was next door.

After I started visiting her clinic regularly, she started noticing the number of patients increasing day by day. One day she told me, "Earlier I would have 40 to 50 patients a day, now it has doubled, sometimes it crosses 120. Money is just flowing, and people are getting better. I have realised all this has occurred since you started visiting my clinic. I am very happy. You keep coming."

I advised her to charge less for the needy and to give them free treatment if needed. I told her she would get back in plenty if she helped the needy.

She agreed and said, "I have noticed the day you don't come, there are very few patients. Some regular patients enquire about you, the day they don't see you. Please come every day."

Her mother, father, and brother all started liking me a lot. They became very close to me and would sometimes come to visit me in her clinic for a few minutes.

While collecting the blood samples from the patients for some tests, just looking at the vial, I would predict what the reports would be, and sometimes even their blood group.

I would have a look at the vials and urine containers kept in the collection box before the lab guy could come and predict the reports. Just by having a look at the urine sample, I was able to tell whether the person was passing pus or blood or if the person had an infection, kidney stones, or any other issue.

She was astonished when I predicted the diagnosis and results, for the first time. I told her, "Be patient, wait till the reports come." In the evening, I entered the clinic exactly at the same time when the lab guy was handing over the reports. She hurriedly opened the reports, was stunned, and confirmed what I said was right. I told her to calm down. This kept happening. Slowly, she got used to it.

Once, a young boy of nine years was brought in an almost unconscious state. I told her, "His sugar is very high. Please check it." She checked it. It was 500+. I guided her to get the boy admitted as soon as possible. The boy was admitted. He got well and was discharged after some days. His parents came along with him to thank us for saving his life. They revealed he was very fond of sweets and chocolates and would eat them throughout the day.

Unbelievable but true, the doctor started asking me for guidance after these experiences. She would ask me what medicines to prescribe for some particular patient to get well soon, giving me a few options. I was just 16 years old then, but somehow names of medicines were shown along with the composition in a vision. I could understand everything and was able to guide her. She became the most famous doctor in the area and would have patients waiting till 11 p.m., sometimes even 11.30 p.m. Earlier, she would close the clinic by 9-9.30 p.m.

She told me, "I will start a lab, you handle it, no one will ask you any questions. Simultaneously, complete your education."

She added, "Actually, I don't think it's needed. You're God-gifted, someone special."

Her mother agreed and told me, "There is something in you, earlier whenever I would have a problem, I would come and take medicines or an injection, but now, spending a few minutes with you, my problems fade. My husband and son feel the same. They have experienced it too."

After three years the doctor's parents got her married to a good guy. She wasn't having kids for a few years even after taking treatment. Once she shared her problem with me.

I told her, "There will be good news soon." I asked her, "When are you expecting your periods?"

She said, "In a few days."

I knew she had already conceived and told her, "Rejoice, your pregnancy is confirmed. You will miss your periods. Do check to be sure."

She confirmed after some days that she was pregnant and thanked me.

I told her, "You will have a boy." She had a boy and was very happy.

The family requested me to name him. They invited me for the naming ceremony. Normally, I don't like to attend functions, unless needed. Here, I did go. Seeing me enter, everyone came to meet me. They made the doctor's husband get up from his seat, made me sit next to her, and gave the baby in my lap. I told them I hadn't carried a baby before. I held the baby for some time and returned it to its mother. I blessed the baby, wished them, and left immediately. Even now, the doctor is still just a call away.

A Life-Changing Moment of Hope and Connection

Around 18 years ago, I received a deeply distressing phone call from the wife of a dear friend. Her voice trembled with desperation as she sobbed uncontrollably. She pleaded with me to come to the hospital immediately, saying her husband had been admitted and was in a critical condition. "He's not responding to treatment or anyone else," she said, her voice filled with fear. I assured her calmly, "I'll come as soon as I can."

Without delay, I contacted another close friend, one of our lifelong companions since our teenage years, and explained the situation. Without hesitation, she agreed to join me. Together, we rushed to the hospital. At the entrance of the ward, his wife was waiting for us, her face etched with worry and exhaustion. The moment she saw me, she urged me to go inside quickly to see her husband, who lay unconscious.

She explained through tears, "He has been in the hospital for the past few days, but since last night, he's stopped responding to treatment. His breathing has become shallow, and the doctors advised me to inform his close ones. I knew you were very close to him, so I called you. Please talk to him. I feel he will respond to you. Only you can save him."

As I absorbed her words, my heart grew heavy. My friend and I walked into the room. She stepped forward first, gently held his hand, and spoke softly to him, but there was no response. Then, I approached his bedside, took his hand in mine, and called out his name firmly. "Open your eyes," I said. "Come back."

To everyone's astonishment, his hand moved slightly. His eyelids flickered, and he gradually opened his eyes halfway, blinking a few times. Though he couldn't speak, his body began to respond. The subtle signs of life brought tears of relief to his wife's eyes. She clasped my hands tightly in gratitude, unable to find the words to thank me. Then, she hurried to call the doctor and nurses.

The medical team arrived promptly, checked his vitals, and confirmed that they were stabilizing. "He's out of danger," the nurse announced a few moments later. The words brought a wave of joy and relief to all of us.

We stayed for some time to ensure he was stable, then left with plans to return the next day. When we visited him again, we were greeted by a beautiful surprise—our friend was up and walking around the ward, looking much better. The sight of him brought immense happiness to all of us, a reminder of the incredible strength of human connection and the power of hope.

Rescuing an Unknown Lady Who Needed Help

Joyfully, I have visited all places of worship, be it a temple, church, mosque, or Gurudwara. Never did I feel one should visit only one place of worship. I remember an incident when I visited a mosque. On my way out, an unknown lady walked up to me and asked for help. She wasn't feeling well, was sweating profusely, couldn't breathe well. She told me, "I was waiting for help. I am not feeling well. Please call my brother, he is an inspector." She handed her mobile to me revealing his name. I helped her to my car. She was in a bad state. Her body was turning cold, still, she repeatedly kept thanking me for the help. She was slipping into an unconscious state. I kept tapping her so that she remained conscious. I called her brother and informed him about her. He advised me to rush her to a hospital and I followed the same. I wheeled her into an emergency unit with the help of my house help and friend. All the while my mother was silently observing me.

Doctors examining her told me, "She had suffered an attack. She is serious. Don't leave till someone from her family comes." I waited and had a thought, "Hope, she regains consciousness, soon and survives the fatal attack."

Silently I kept checking her from a little distance. I saw her responding. After some minutes, one of the doctors who was attending to her came and told me, "She is responding, she is safe now but will require further investigation." I thanked the doctor and informed her brother. Her brother was relieved and thanked me. He was on duty, came in, and took charge of the situation. He said, "She didn't inform anyone at home about visiting a mosque. I am surprised to hear this. It seems from the office she directly went there." He requested me to note down his number and told me, "If you anytime need any help, without thinking, please call. I will take care of my sister now. Thank you for your timely help." We then left for home

I love animals, birds, and plants. Some of my healing experiences with plants and animals are:

Healing of Plants

I had shifted to a new place on rent. I had many plants like the hibiscus, pink and white coloured, kadipatta, ajwain, aloe vera, and a few herbs. A few days after I shifted, the watchman came and informed me, "According to society's rules, plants are not allowed to be kept in the balcony." Before shifting, I had spoken to the broker and had asked him to enquire about the society's rules. The broker had told me, "Plants are allowed to be kept in the balcony." After the watchman conveyed the message, I called my broker. He said, "The society must have changed the rules."

I felt cheated but didn't say anything. I was immediately shown he would be punished sometime later, not only for this but, for other things too.

All the plants had grown beautifully, and I didn't know what to do. I couldn't find anyone who I could give them to. Slowly the plants started dying one by one. I felt very hurt seeing them die, and decided, "I will never buy any plant till I have a house of my own, also will make sure that there is society's permission."

I loved the kadipatta plant the most, as I had bought it when it was a very tiny sapling, smaller than my little finger, with a few leaves. It had grown large and so had the ajwain plant.

Over time, all the plants died. I emptied all the pots except the one with the kadipatta and ajwain. Almost six months passed, and there were only dry stalks of kadipatta and ajwain in the pot. When I touched the stalks of kadipatta and ajwain to check, they crumbled, as I hadn't watered them for months.

One afternoon, I had a thought: "I should try healing the plant. Will I be able to revive the plants? Is it possible?" With a lot of compassion and positive thoughts, I poured water and sat beside the pot. I started sending healing energy while I talked to the plants.

I could feel the plants receiving the energy happily. I was sure now that the plants would spring back to life. I did it for two more days. Miraculously, within two days a small sapling and tiny leaves of kadipatta could be seen. I was on cloud nine seeing the dead plant grow again after almost six months.

After a few days, the ajwain plant started growing too. It got tiny new leaves, that too without sunlight. I couldn't believe my eyes. Later on, I placed the pot near the window, inside the house, where it got a bit of sunlight. The plants grew big. The leaves were much greener and fresher than the original plant.

By then, I happened to meet an aunt who ran a restaurant of her own next to my building. I gave the plants to her. She happily accepted them and kept them in the compound.

She later told me, "The fragrance of ajwain and kadipatta leaves are too good, not like the ones we get from the market. I use them in dishes, especially dal, and the taste is very nice."

She also added, "I noted a change in my business. After accepting the plants from you and adding kadipatta leaves to the dal, the dish was in demand and sold in different variations. My business is doing very well. I had to hire more cooks and delivery guys." I just smiled and, over time, healed her too.

Healing of Animals

In 2017, before being initiated into Kundalini Meditation, I had once gone to meet an aunt, the one who runs a restaurant. While we were chatting, a man hurriedly came in and asked her whether she knew any veterinarian. He was pleading with her to recommend someone as his 3-year-old Labrador was having a high fever of 105 °F. He had taken his pet dog to the doctor, but the doctor had already left for the day; it was afternoon, and there were no vets available. I offered to help him. I told him to bring in his dog. He carried his dog from the car. The dog was almost unconscious, and his mouth was frothing. I wiped his froth and started giving him healing. The dog showed improvement, and his temperature became normal within a few minutes.

The owner of the dog checked the temperature and said, "It's normal." The dog got up, waged his tail, and started playing. The owner of the dog thanked me, blessed me, and wished me the best for saving his Labrador. I was so happy to see him healed.

I used to visit this aunt for a few minutes, after walks, as she loved to spend time with me. She was surprised to see the dog's recovery.

During this time, there was a stray dog who used to come to her restaurant every day, any time of the day. I had seen him. One day when I went to visit her, he came to her place in a bad state, injured. He stood at the entrance looking at me, asking for help. It seemed as if some dogs had attacked him. I went close to him. Aunty was scared looking at his condition, thinking he had gone mad, and tried to shoo him off with a stick. I told her not to do it and let me see him.

The dog had not been visiting her place for a few days, lately. I saw his wound, and a large chunk of flesh from his back had been ripped off. But he allowed me to touch him. I kept looking at the wound and sent energy for a while, bought a small pack of pedigree food, fed him, and gave him water. He happily wagged his tail; ate the food, and drank water. I could see gratitude in his eyes. He then went away.

The next day again I went at the same time to see him. I was sure he would come. He came immediately after I reached. I did the same thing for three days. On the 3rd day, his wound appeared dry, and within a few days, he was fine. After, healing him, the dog started coming to this aunt's place to meet me, always happily wagging his tail. He was a local dog but somehow would get a whiff that I had come. I used to pet him and feed him every day at the same time after walks. This carried on till the lockdown.

The First Meeting with My Guru

My mother and I attended a spiritual retreat with thousands of participants. It was my first spiritual retreat ever. I fell sick within a few hours of attending it, and this problem thus paved the path to meet my enlightened master.

I met Poojya Guruji on 9/1/2010 for the first time. He opened the door with a smile and said, "Come, I was waiting for you. From the moment your husband called up, I was waiting for you. I didn't sleep properly, was waiting for you, Come." He introduced himself as a Preventive Health Plan Consultant, and for many years I would address him as 'uncle.'

Later on, after many years, he said that my marriage was not supposed to happen. It happened for a reason.

On The First Day of My Healing

Uncle confirmed there is always a divine presence with me. He looked at my palms and said, "Any which ways you would have reached me. You are a pure soul. Tell me, what's your problem?"

I told him, "Uncle, my urine has stopped, and I am passing pus and blood instead of urine. I am also passing blood in my stools. No doctors are able to treat me. I went through a major surgery, due to the doctors' negligence. After two years, again I had to go through a surgical procedure."

He asked me why was it done. I told him doctors told my mother that if I didn't get operated within two or three days, I would die within a month.

Uncle revealed what I never told him before. He said, "The doctors have cheated you; You were perfectly ok. From there, your health problems have started." As he was revealing this to me, I could see clearly how the doctors had fooled us and how I wasn't willing to get operated.

He continued, "They have done wrong, they will suffer. But there is no need to worry."

He asked me, when was I operated. I replied, "11 years back." He said, "You are lucky, you will get to see all, those who cause you trouble, being punished." I said, "Yes, I have seen it."

He consoled, "Don't worry. You will be fine."

He smiled. He further predicted that I would become a healer. He looked at my palms and said, "It is 100% sure."

Uncle made me do Jalneti and said, "Very good, have you learnt yoga? The water is passing so easily." He then told me to see a video on his laptop, it was about self-healing and Jalneti. He told me to heal myself continuously. He taught me how to heal.

He gave me healing for severe UTI and the unbearable pain in the abdomen; while healing, I felt vibrations; and a heavy flow of energy throughout my body; tears kept flowing, and I couldn't understand why. I was healed instantly.

He then said, "The house where you live is not good." This was the house before I moved to the haunted house.

Uncle told me to go to the washroom after healing. To my surprise, I passed urine that was crystal clear without blood, pus, or even pain.

He told me, "Never go to such retreats with huge crowds, as there will be a lot of negativity, and it will affect you. Also, avoid going out after it becomes dark, going to religious places when it is crowded. For others it won't matter; since you are pure, your energy will be absorbed by unwanted people. Also don't talk much to people, keep your talk minimum. Don't waste your energy. People will try to talk to you, especially after understanding the benefit they receive after talking to you."

He looked at my palms and told me, "Very nice palms. You are so full of love, so much compassion, and very pure. You can become healthy and become a healer. You are a very pure soul and have never done wrong to anyone. Your health issues started after the surgery. Your friends and family are not good; practice detachment from them, or they will keep hurting you. You have done a lot for others, now take care of yourself and be happy. You have zero resistance."

He gave me a chart with instructions to follow: have juices, avoid cold drinks, ice creams, chocolates, do self-healing continuously, exercise, and acupressure. He told me to be happy.

He advised me to light a lamp and to keep it burning continuously, which I did. It continues to burn. He didn't reveal the purpose of lighting the lamp nor did I ask him. After many years of meditation, one day I received an insight that it is for all Gurus. By lighting it, I am connected to them. It has been continuously burning for more than 15 years since I met Guruji.

He said, "Your blood is impure."

I used to drink less water. After the first healing, he advised me to have lots of water, tender coconut water, and barley water. I strictly followed his advice.

After my first healing, which was instantly successful, I had a silent wish to heal others. My blood was purified within a few healings.

Uncle even told me many times that in my case doctors will never be able to diagnose my health problems.

He gave me four beads of coral and asked me to keep them with me always, he even told me, "You can put them around your neck so that they won't get lost." The beads were very small and had tiny holes, I passed a thread through the beads and wore it around my neck. After some days, the thread kept snapping and beads kept falling. One day they kept falling continuously so I removed and kept them and went for a bath. When I came back, they had disappeared. I told him about it and asked him whether I should buy new ones. He smiled and said, "There's no need." He gave me a book written by him.

After my first healing, I came to know about his healing powers, after I was cured instantly of the problems that I was facing. I would wonder, "Why some people called him Guruji?" Many years later I came to know he was an enlightened master. Once he told me, "Buy a good phone. I want to add you to WhatsApp group." At that time, I was using a simple phone. I just nodded, somehow I managed to buy a second-hand phone, and happily, I went to meet him to let him know, that he could now add me to WhatsApp. On meeting him I happily told him, "Uncle, I have bought a phone, now you can add me to WhatsApp." The best part here was, instead of I surprising him he surprised me. He smiled and answered, just check your phone, I have already added you. He hugged me and said, "Now you can message me even when I am not in India. When I am in India, you can call or message anytime."

On the Second Day of My Healing

Uncle asked me my name, to which I replied, "Shashtria." He paused for a few seconds and said, "I don't know whatever your name may be. From today on, I will call you Sruthi." I asked him, "What does Sruthi mean?"

He said, "In Sanskrit, it means revelation." He looked at my palms and said, "You have lots of support."

I didn't understand then, but now I do understand; he meant it was astral support.

He also said, "You had strong Divine help before meeting me. You still have it. You have lots of Punya; you will easily come out of all the problems. You also have lots of money."

I said, "I don't have any money. I gave away most of my earnings to the needy. Whatever little savings I had, it got over while taking care of my mom."

He said, "Money will come; lots will come. It's there in your palms."

He then told me to go and stand behind the closed door, the main door. I wondered why he was telling me this. Was it a punishment?

I went and stood as asked. He instantly said, "Very nice aura. Come, come soon."

I didn't understand what it meant, nor did I ask him.

He further added, "According to your palms, you should have been dead long back and should have been six feet under the ground. I don't know how you are surviving. You are a living miracle. I salute you.

It is impossible for anyone to survive with what you are going through. Your gratitude overflows. You are so full of love, I cannot say. See, see your palms."

I looked at my palms but didn't understand a bit. I asked him, "May I learn palm reading?"

Uncle said, "No need, don't worry. Do not depend on palms; we can change our destiny to a certain extent. You have strong willpower; you can change your life, and you can overcome everything with ease. You have a lot of grace. In this life, you have only Punya."

He then shared lots of things about me which I am guided not to share. Uncle also told me, "You have to be careful of jealousy. Detach yourself from everyone. Your friends and many people are jealous of you. It is very bad. Jealousy can pull down a person or even cause death."

I told him, "I don't have anything, still?"

He said, "You have everything. Everything will be shown to you at the right time. Your purpose will be shown to you. You have lots of support. Fame is there in your hands."

Uncle taught me a way to protect myself.

He then revealed, "There is a tumour in your head which has to go." He took a pen, made a few circles on my palm, and taught me to heal my head. To be sure, my ex got my MRI done for me. The MRI report of the brain didn't show any tumour. Guruji explained diseases remain in the astral body before entering the physical body. The tumour hadn't formed in my brain. He confirmed I got rid of it with my efforts of self-healing.

He used to call and check my health. He would tell me his travel plans and he asked me to be on Facebook so he could connect when he was abroad.

I replied, "I don't have a Facebook account."

To this, he said, "Don't worry, you can connect to me anytime, anywhere." Recently, things unfolded as to why he had said it, then. Though I was not aware, I realised I could travel astrally, only when he said it.

On the Third Day of Healing

On the third day of my healing, he told me, "The activities that are taking place in your house, tell the place is haunted." He advised me to leave the house, saying it was not good. Once again, he revealed a lot more things.

The Haunted House

About 11 years ago, we moved into a rented apartment. (This was after Guruji had told us to shift from the earlier flat). Shortly after settling in, I started observing some strange paranormal activities, like some presence in the house, in fact, more than one. The gas knob would automatically be switched on and there would be a gas leak, loud noise of the vessels falling would be heard and on checking, would find everything was placed rightly. Food grains, pulses, flour, all foodstuffs, within some time, would get infested with insects. There were noises and movements in the wardrobe, banging on the windows late at night, movements in the above flat throughout the day and night, and much more. Initially, I was hesitant to tell anyone. I then spoke to my mother and my husband about it. My mother came to stay with me permanently, and she too confirmed, it was true.

Things began to get from bad to worse. My health started deteriorating. Thrice we did some procedures for my heart, and all of them failed. Though the devices (such as Holter monitor and V-Patch) showed fault and doctors would plan surgery, just whenever I was on the operation table on the day of surgery, during the procedure my heart showed no abnormalities despite being given injections to trigger my heart and to find fault to finish the problem. The doctors would get confused. The moment I was at home, my heartbeat would again fluctuate. My mother and ex too had daily experienced abnormal activities during the day and night.

I would often be hospitalised and ended up in an ICU for various issues- mostly high BP and heart issues very high heart beats SVT. uncle kept healing me. But as soon as I entered the house, my energy was sapped immediately. At times I had no energy even to stand. I would get up with the support of the wall and walk. Every night I would be dragged out of my bed and would find myself on the cold floor. Many spirits were in the house, and I could see and experience their presence.

I had all the problems, right from head to toe: high blood pressure, brain clot, heart issues, gall bladder, eyes, urinary tract infections, three heart procedures similar to angioplasty, brain stroke, one side of my body had gone weak, and I wasn't able to even pick up a cup, severe vertigo, heavy bleeding for many days, fibroids, and thus severe weakness. Things kept happening one after the other in the haunted flat.

The most painful part was being diagnosed with SVT -Supraventricular Tachycardia. The symptoms were overwhelming - difficulty breathing, the sensation of impending death, numbness in my extremities, fainting spells, vomiting, and an uncontrollable urge to pass urine and stool simultaneously.

I was hospitalized numerous times and underwent several procedures. Despite extensive testing, including the attachment of event recorders for varying durations; the doctors couldn't detect any abnormalities. Even with beta-blockers, SVT attacks persisted, leaving both me and my cardiologist perplexed. Despite his best efforts, the cause remained elusive.

Once, I was thrown out of bed in the middle of the night and hurt my head. My blood pressure shot up to 180/120, and my pulse was 190. I couldn't speak; I had lost my voice and collapsed. I was immediately rushed to a hospital and taken to the ICU. The brain MRI was done, and it showed a clot. I had suffered a brain stroke.

After an hour, I opened my eyes. I had an Ischemic stroke at 2 a.m. due to very high heartbeats (SVT) and couldn't talk at all. The right side of my body suddenly became weak. I prayed, and I immediately received Divine energy and felt Divine presence with me. After two hours, I was able to speak and was discharged the next day. The doctors were surprised when I was able to speak in the morning.

After a few days when I went to uncle for healing, I asked him about the clot. He smilingly said, "You can talk now, the clot may have disappeared till now."

When I started having heart issues in the haunted flat, I asked uncle, "Do I have a weak heart? I have read your holy book; it says, 'People with weak hearts can foresee future happenings.'"

Uncle said, "No, your case is different; you will be able to see things." I had told him, "Whatever I think happens." Uncle said, "Yes, it will happen."

In the same house, I suddenly got an eye infection. I couldn't see properly. I was in intense pain, and my eyes had become red, while there was a continuous discharge from my eyes. My family asked me to go to an ophthalmologist. The doctor gave me some drops for 15 days, and it worsened my eyesight.

I took another doctor's opinion, and the doctor said, "I had developed cataracts due to the drops (steroids) given to me."

Uncle gave me healing and told me to splash my urine in my eyes and do self-healing. The eye infection was cleared in three days.

Another incident was when I started having unbearable pain in my stomach. When I did a sonography, it showed gallstones in the gall bladder. The doctor said an immediate surgery would be required.

I told uncle about the report, and he called me for healing. He said, "After healing you can get operated. It's a small surgery, or you can even manage with self-healing."

I did self-healing continuously and the pain disappeared within a month. Divine grace saved me from all the hurdles that came my way.

Once, after healing, uncle made me sit with him and said, "You tell me your problems. Why are you keeping quiet? You must tell me." I just looked at him and didn't say a single word.

Uncle then revealed, "Your building is built on a graveyard. The entire area is built on a graveyard. I can challenge you: wherever you dig, you will find skeletons. You should leave the house immediately. It's a miracle to survive in that house. From now on, nothing will affect you."

On the last day of shifting from the haunted house, I found out that a lady had committed suicide in the flat above us. After leaving the haunted house, I slowly recovered.

Days With Uncle During Healings

Sometimes, uncle would make juices and make sure I had it. Once, I asked him "Which juice is this?" He said, "Don't ask just have it" and he would stand beside me till I finished it.

I remember during the initial days when I met uncle, he asked me something and while I was answering uncle advised, "Use small words; I can understand."

He smiled and said, "Make some mistakes. You are very intelligent. Hide your intelligence. Do not show it to anyone. People will be jealous of you. If someone tries to show you, they know everything, you only keep quiet and listen, let them talk, behave like a buddhu (fool). You have all the knowledge; It will be shown to you at the right time. It is there in your hands."

From that very moment, my way of writing or speaking completely changed, and I toned myself making it very simple. Uncle looked at my palms and said, "You can be a good writer; start writing."

I asked uncle, "What should I write?" He said, "You can write anything."

Much later, in meditation, I was shown the answer as to why uncle had told me to keep my speech and writing simple.

In retrospect, I remember, I was always praised for my write-ups and essays. My mother's brother who resides in Dubai still has handwritten letters which I used to write to him when I was a child.

He told my mother, "Your daughter writes so well. I have preserved all the letters."

On a few occasions, uncle had asked me to share my life with some patients who had come for healing. Here are two such incidents I shared.

One was of a girl having a brain tumour. She had come from abroad to receive uncle's divine healing. Doctors couldn't give her a solution. She was depressed and had given up on life. uncle asked me to talk to her, guide her, and also to share a bit of my life experiences. After speaking to me, she was happy, smiling, and wished to be in touch with me. Uncle was very happy to see her smiling.

The second incident was of a lady telling uncle about ghosts in her house. I had finished my healing from uncle and was about to leave. Uncle held my hand, took me near them, and told me to wait and explain to them what it is to live with real ghosts. He told her and her family members, "Ask her: she will tell you what real ghosts are, and how bravely she is facing the situation alone."

I explained to them in brief. They were very scared hearing just a few incidents.

Uncle said, "You can't even imagine what she is going through because of the negative energies in her house. The building is built on a graveyard. It is impossible to survive there."

He then told me, "Life has been very unfair to you." He told them, "She is a very nice girl, very pure. She has no Karmas; still, she is bearing everything very patiently. See, how she is still smiling."

I remember uncle telling me, "You have strong willpower. You can change your life."

The Elephant Hair

Once, after uncle left for Kerala, one Tuesday, as I was about to enter the Siddhivinayak temple a man who resembled uncle stopped me at the entrance. He was dressed in a white cotton dhoti and kurta. He had a string of beads around his neck like a japmala, and wore a U-shaped chandan tilak with a vertical line inside, similar to those on deity idols. He carried a creamish-white cotton shoulder bag and told me to wait, saying he had brought something for me all the way from Kerala. When he mentioned Kerala, I looked at him in awe, wondering if he could be uncle himself.

He spoke fluent English, was very polite and soft-spoken, and maintained a smile throughout. He asked if I came to the temple every Tuesday, to which I replied affirmatively. He insisted that I accept an elephant hair, describing it as very auspicious.

At one point, I even considered if he could be uncle's twin brother, but then I questioned why uncle's brother would come to Mumbai just to give me a strand of elephant hair. However, I hesitated and told him that I didn't know him well enough to accept such a gift.

I offered to pay him, which he refused. Instead, he gave me two strands of elephant hair and suggested that I have them made into a gold ring by a trusted jeweller, recommending a specific shop.

He then mentioned he would meet me the following Tuesday before leaving. After our temple visit, he bid farewell to me with a smile. Later, my friend from Kerala and I had the elephant hair verified at a jeweller's shop, confirming its authenticity.

Next Tuesday when we reached the Siddhivinayak temple, my friend suggested that we observe him from a distance for a few minutes. My friend too was keen on acquiring elephant hair strands.

We watched the man standing patiently, seemingly waiting for someone, without engaging or interacting with anyone else. After a while, my friend suggested we leave, advising me not to look at him and implying he might be trying to deceive me.

The man was positioned near the temple entrance and as I walked past, he called out to me, saying, "Listen." His voice resembled uncle's. I immediately turned back, and he greeted me with a smile, asking how I was. We exchanged pleasantries and then I mentioned to him that I had told my friends about him, and they were interested in acquiring elephant hair too. They were willing to pay any amount for it. I inquired if he had any available.

He angrily looked at my friend and strictly said "No, I can't give you. I don't have anything to give to your friends. Don't give anyone, what I gave you. I came all the way from Kerala only to meet you and am going back today. May be someday you will come to Kerala." Saying this, he left hurriedly

He glanced back once, smiled and disappeared into the crowd.

When I later shared this with uncle, he confirmed it was him and advised me to keep the elephant hair safe, as it was very auspicious.

I still have the hair, ring, and gold coin that I received from one of the priests of Siddhivinayak temple.

From Uncle to Guru: A Divine Transition

In May 2018, uncle happily welcomed me and took me to his healing room. He asked me to lie down for healing. Just then, he remembered something and told me "Wait, I will come." I was alone in the healing room, and thoughts began to come: "I am breathing normally. Why is uncle telling me to correct my breathing? What is wrong with my breathing? Am I breathing incorrectly?" I never ever had breathing issues. Till uncle was away, I began to experiment my breathing count, at one point I could hold my breath easily for 14 seconds. I kept experimenting till he came.

The same day, after receiving the last healing I asked uncle, "When can I see you?" With a sparkle in his eyes, he said, "Why do you want to see me? You are strong and can grow on your own. Correct your breathing."

Without realising what he said about breathing, I don't know why I said, "Ok Guruji."

It was the first time ever I had said Guruji to him. From day one, I called him uncle. After saying it I wondered, how did I say it? What will he say? I never had a spiritual Guru before Guruji and never longed for one.

On hearing me address him as "Guruji" for the very first time, Poojya Guruji smiled. His eyes became moist, and he was very happy. He hugged me and blessed me.

On my way back home, I wondered "Why did he say not to meet him.? Did I do something wrong?" Silently, I cried the entire journey back home and kept wiping my tears, not letting the auto guy know that I was crying.

My heart felt heavy and at that very moment a thought came to my mind, "he cares for you, whatever he has done, he has done for your good." I realised that there are many who need him more than me. I should do my part without disturbing him. I always accepted everything as it is.

Strengthening My Inner Self

After reaching home, I remembered Guruji's words. I picked up his book and began to read. Slowly, I began to follow the breathing count, pranayama, and mastered the art of breathing with grace.

I had quit everything like ice cream, chocolates, cakes, sweets, cold drinks, cold water, fried food, papads, pickles, bakery products, and many more things, that Guruji had told me to quit and I followed each of his instructions clearly, from the very first day I met him in 2010. Guruji had permitted me to have a cup of coffee daily.

In 2018, a few months before my initiation, he messaged me to stop milk, milk products, and sugar. I wondered why did he say it now. Why did he not say it on the first day of meeting him? Instantly, I promised him that I would never touch the above things. Within no time, I quit coffee, milk, milk products, and sugar. I haven›t touched it till today. I completely stopped all outside food, even those which were allowed. I consumed only homemade food cooked by myself.

Divine grace, self-healing, and Guruji's constant guidance helped me overcome my health issues and prepared me for a deeper spiritual path. Pomegranate juice has brought a lot of changes in me. Pomegranate juice is prepared with fruit, outer cover, and pomegranate seeds

Through Kundalini meditation, I found my true self and the purpose of my life. I experienced multiple Kundalini awakenings, each one stirring something deep inside. I felt energy gushing through me, that was unexplainable.

I started healing people with Guruji's permission. After a few years, Guruji told me, "From Now on, you can heal people of all diseases," and that was a turning point. At the moment I felt my childhood wish to heal others was being manifested.

I have had the privilege of helping people overcome illnesses that seemed impossible to cure. When patients come back and share their stories of recovery, the joy I feel is beyond words. It's not just relief or pride—it's an overwhelming sense of gratitude to be chosen by Nature to bring this kind of light to others.

For me, healing is not just about treating an illness or curing someone. It's about connecting with someone's spirit, lifting them, and offering them a solution. Every time someone finds health, hope, or even a little harmony through this divine gift I've been given, I feel Divine grace that guided me to this path. I am blessed to be able to do this work.

As far as my health was concerned, I understood self-healing is essential for my overall well-being and quality of life. I could concentrate and work on the underlying issues that affected me, emotionally, mentally, and physically.

Self-healing made me deal not only with my pain but made me proactive towards nurturing myself.

I worked on myself, and I started having experiences within some days.

My Self-Healing experiences

At times, I had been experiencing heat and the flow of energy in my hands for a few days. The moment I kept my hand on any part of my body during self-healing, I could feel the heat and energy passing through. Sometimes high energy was felt while healing.

While doing self-healing, I felt heavy vibrations there was a lot of heat generated and I could feel myself getting better with Divine grace. Afterwards, the heat was reduced to a great extent, and I was feeling much better, getting stronger day by day. On a Thursday during group meditation, I felt a lot of energy entering through the Sahasrara Chakra while doing self-healing. I was receiving energy (it appeared as light) through the Sahasrara Chakra while doing self-healing daily.

Previously, when I would heal my hands would get hot, even now they get hot and I also feel energy (like an electric current) at the tips of my fingers. Also, if I have pain anywhere in my body, it reduces within a few minutes.

My self-healing and Om Shanti chanting, instead of painkiller

I was very scared of dental treatment, had left my treatment incomplete in my teens, and never visited a dentist. With continuous chanting of "Om Shanti", I started my dental treatment there was one root canal and four very deep fillings to be done. I kept chanting Om Shanti mentally, though there was swelling, I didn't have any pain and had no painkillers.

I got it done a few months back before the lockdown with no painkillers, chanting "OM Shanti" and Self-healing helped me, the doctor told me "You will have pain so we will give some gaps."

When I met the doctor for the next appointment, he asked me "Did you have the tablets which I prescribed." I told him, "As advised by you I bought it, as you had told me not to take a chance as the pain would be unbearable and that you would not be there for a few days. I didn't have any" and showed him the medicine strips. He was surprised to know I hadn't taken a single tablet, and I had no pain.

Jalneti and Self-healing for my wounded eye

One night, while trying to retrieve hangers holding dry clothes from a high clothesline, an empty metal hanger slipped and hit my eye, causing internal bleeding. Surprisingly, I felt no pain or discomfort. Just then, I heard a notification sound. It was Guruji's message on our group: "Do Jalneti." Generally, Guruji doesn't message so late, immediately I did Jalneti. He had told me "Do Jalneti whenever you feel negativity is affecting you." I focused on healing my eye. The bleeding ceased, and a clot could be seen.

My aunt and her daughter, who had been staying with me for a month, were concerned and urged me to see a doctor. Aware that it was Sunday, and clinics would likely be closed, I was guided to go anyway.

We found an auto rickshaw and asked the driver to take us to a doctor, as I wasn't familiar with local healthcare options. He took us to a hospital where a specialist happened to be visiting. After examining my eye, he reassured me that it was badly injured but not a serious issue like a corneal injury. He advised me to apply ice and consult an ophthalmologist the next morning.

He reassured me not to worry and did not charge any fees for the consultation.

When I woke up the next morning after the incident, I performed Jalneti and continued with self-healing practices, after experiencing a peaceful night's sleep. I visited an ophthalmologist. During the examination, he checked my eyes thoroughly, including a retina check, and asked if I felt any pain or discomfort. I assured him I had felt none, even at the time of the injury the previous day. I had come as a precautionary measure based on the specialist's recommendation and my family's concern.

After examining my eye, the ophthalmologist informed me that I had suffered a haemorrhage of the sclera (the white part of the eye). He expressed amazement and gratitude, lifting his hands towards the sky, noting that my cornea had narrowly escaped damage. He assured me that the clot and blood spots would gradually dissipate.

He inquired about my daily routine, and I shared with him that I practice meditation daily and had performed healing on myself both that day and the day before, confident that there was no cause for concern.

He asked me about my medical history. I mentioned having had high blood pressure issues for nearly 20 years, but it was no longer a concern. The ophthalmologist positively noted that despite this history, my retina showed no signs of damage, which reassured him. I credited this to the blessings and protection of my Guruji. He also asked about the type of meditation I practice, to which I mentioned Kundalini Meditation.

The ophthalmologist expressed his respect with a gesture of pranams and remarked that he was very pleased to meet someone as positive and brave as me. He prescribed two types of eyedrops for me to use over the next five days.

Rare and Cherished Moments with Guruji

I feel Guruji's presence every Thursday from the first Thursday we started group meditation. After Thursday meditation Guruji gave me his blessing, and while leaving I saw him reducing himself (very tiny) and leaving.

There was a lot of heat generated in my body. The soles of my feet felt hot. I wrote to Guruji asking for guidance. Soon after our Thursday group meditation, the problem of heat on the soles got solved (Group meditation is a meditation conducted by Guruji for all our group meditation members at a specific time every Thursday morning). Every Thursday, during our meditation, I felt an intense flow of energy during the first or last few minutes. The feeling is unexplainable, and I am also able to get the darshan of our beloved Guruji. Sometimes he waits for me to open my eyes, gives me blessings on my head, and then leaves. It has now become almost a daily occurrence of him giving me morning darshan after meditation.

While writing my experiences, I had his Holy Book beside me. After writing, I looked at his Holy Book to thank him, and surprisingly his photo appeared live for a few minutes as if he was looking at me and smiling. I felt blessed.

Meeting Guruji in Feb 2022 at his residence

In Feb 2022, I received an insight during meditation to meet Guruji. After some days, again I got an indication from someone close to me to meet Guruji. Since it was the second time. I asked Guruji if I could meet him. He said "Yes."

When I went to meet him, a member of my meditation group also joined me. While talking to me Guruji checked my palms and said, "Your brain tumour has gone, and in that place, a protection has been formed. Actually, a double protection has been formed. You don't have any health issues now. You are strong. There is nothing to worry." I was very happy and thanked him.

At Hyderabad Retreat with Guruji

A triangle formed on the island Guruji had once drawn on my palm within these three days. Since then, many have been formed.

Guruji told me that all my blocks have cleared, and I don't have to take any medicines hereafter. That, I will keep getting Kundalini awakening.

I was so thrilled and relieved at the same time. I was in total bliss.

At Kannur Retreat with Guruji

Once during the Kannur retreat, Guruji joined us for dinner and told me, "You must give back to everyone who troubles you." I said, "Guruji, you know that's what I can't do, I couldn't do it earlier too." He said, "No, you must give back, not to tolerate." I replied, "I still can't do it. I can't hurt anyone." He smiled.

At Udaipur Retreat with Guruji

At our Udaipur retreat, when I met Guruji, he was very happy. He took me aside and told me, "Since many members are jealous of you and want to be where you have reached, I had to tell a member lies that your experiences are not real. She was troubling me. She was very cunning, and she recorded my words and sent them to many members.

Don't worry. I did it to protect you from jealousy." I told Guruji, "I forgave her." He told me, "Very good; I love you," and then he said again, "You don't worry."

At the second Hyderabad Retreat with Guruji

My near ones were insisting I take the vaccine. I told them my Guruji had told me not to take it. They didn't listen or believe me and asked me to write to Guruji for guidance before travelling to Hyderabad. Since they weren't listening to me, before our Hyderabad retreat, hesitatingly, I wrote to Guruji asking him if I should take the vaccine.

After messaging Guruji, instantly I could hear his voice in my ears, saying "You need not take it. Your vibrations are high. Even if the virus enters, it will not be able to sustain itself. Not to worry."

I told my near ones, "My Guruji has replied. His guidance was the same- No need to take the vaccine." They insisted, but I was firm on my decision. I did the RTPCR test before leaving for Hyderabad and asked the airlines about the rules. They said, "If not vaccinated, an RTPCR negative report is compulsory. We have the data of all passengers, those who have taken the vaccine and those who haven't. Please carry the RTPCR report."

I kept my reports ready at the airport, No one asked or checked the reports while going or while coming back. I made sure to get my RTPCR done before my journeys, following the airline rules.

Till today I have not taken the COVID-19 vaccine and have travelled alone without any fear.

At Visakhapatnam Retreat with Guruji

During the Visakhapatnam retreat, we were all seeking Guruji's blessings. When my turn came, Guruji happily smiled and said, "What do I give you? You have Krishna with you. You have everything. You will keep getting in abundance." He then blessed me.

I looked at him but didn't understand what he meant then. Now I do. The same day, I told Guruji, "I keep getting kundalini awakenings."

Guruji said "It's correct. You will keep getting it. In fact, now you can heal all diseases, except Corona. Do not heal anyone with Corona, as it is negative energy. If you heal, all the diseases that have gone from you will come back again. Do not heal."

I stood dazed listening to his precious words. With divine grace, guidance, blessings, and permissions, since a year back, I have healed members of our group and a few more people. Some get healed instantly after calling me.

Guruji had also told me, "You can reach wherever you want. You will keep meeting higher Gurus and you have to accept them. You are at a very high level, and you can create whatever you want."

Meditation Experiences Before My Initiation

I was guided by a deity to meditate. I bought my meditation mat and began meditating on my own. I was shown the exact shop, from where the mat was to be bought. When I began meditating for the first time ever, I could feel I had done this before. It was easy. I felt the same during my initiation.

Every day, just a little before dawn, I could hear a flute playing in the haunted house I lived in. Soon after, Divine would come and gently lift me from my sleep and make me sit, indicating me to meditate. This divine wake-up call continued until I could rise naturally. Now, I am woken up this way only on Thursdays.

When I first sat down to meditate, it felt I had done it before; my breathing was effortless, and I began having experiences long before my initiation.

In my second experience, while meditating, tears started rolling down my cheeks. There was something happening within which I couldn't understand.

I continued meditating. My eyes were wet even after my meditation was over. I would go blank while meditating. There were no thoughts at all. Over time, my breathing improved.

My meditation journey began long before I was initiated. I had raised my Kundalini many times before initiation and had multiple divine interventions. Over time, I've been blessed with the guidance and blessings of many revered Gurus, including Sri Yukteshwar, Adi Shankaracharya, Ramana Maharshi, Mahavatar Babaji, Lahiri Mahasaya, Vivekananda, Paramhansa Yogananda, Ved Vyasa, Chanakya, Agastya, and Bhagwan Nityananda (Ganeshpuri), Vishwamitra, Vashistha, Saint John Bosco, Mother Teresa, Ravana, countless gods, Goddesses, saints, and many more, some were Japanese or Chinese too, the names were shown to me while meditating. I don't know any of them but remembered the names shown and wrote down some of the names after my meditation was over

Among these divine experiences, I've also felt the presence and received blessings and protection of archangels Gabriel, Michael, and Raphael, along with countless Gods and Goddesses whose names were previously unknown to me. I've always approached these experiences with an open heart, letting them flow without clinging to them.

I began documenting my experiences only after Guruji guided me to do so, affirming that all my experiences were valid and encouraging me to note them down. I share them on our meditation group, only when directed. Guruji had asked me to share my life's journey in our meditation group. I jot down my experiences and then let them go. There are times when no experiences occur at all.

I had never actively sought a Guru, nor did I understand the concepts of initiation or meditation.

When our group admin posted in our meditation group about the first and second-level Kundalini Meditation initiation, I didn't know what it meant. I had a feeling, I too should be initiated, so when she posted again, I requested her to add my name to the first-level initiation. She added my name. The joy I felt upon receiving her confirmation was inexplicable.

The Sacred Process of Initiation

My First Initiation: 11th October, Thursday 2018 at 11 am

During my initiation into the first level of Kundalini meditation, Guruji began to explain the breathing techniques, the vibrations, and the movements we might experience during the practice. He mentioned, "Do not be afraid."

I was already feeling those vibrations as Guruji spoke. I shared with him that I was experiencing these sensations, and it felt like a beautiful synchronicity between his teachings and my personal experience.

On the day of my first-level initiation, Guruji assured me that all my chakras were clear.

I never skipped meditation after being initiated and I am following everything as guided without fail. I have made no mistakes.

At one time, I was meditating five times a day. Gradually, I began experiencing various phenomena, which I shared with our Param Poojya Guruji, unsure of their significance. Guruji advised me to post my experiences in our meditation group platform.

My Second Level Initiation: August 1, 2019

On the day of my second level initiation, during my morning meditation, I was graced by Lord Shiva in many different forms. His blessings were profoundly felt.

Throughout the initiation, I experienced intense vibrations in all my chakras. I shared these sensations with Guruji, who guided us to breathe through each chakra. I found myself able to breathe effortlessly through all of them. The experience was beyond words.

I was initiated into Kundalini Meditation, and I realised my soul has taken physical form for a reason and each day is a new birth for me. During my teenage days, my friends tried to deviate my path, but I stayed strong, fought all odds, and still survived.

I was sure I am here for a purpose. God has kept me alive for a reason. Today, with divine grace I am aware of my purpose and doing the best that I can with the abundance of blessings that I keep on receiving.

The toughest part was after being initiated. I faced a lot of obstacles in my spiritual journey, but I kept going and still continued my practice morning and evening without fail. I used to follow a strict routine, began to get up very early and meditate during Brahma Muhurat, and I still continue to do.

My First Kundalini Awakening

My first Kundalini rising was much before I was initiated.

While meditating, I experienced vibrations near the Mooladhara Chakra and felt energy moving upwards through the Sushumna Nadi. The energy reached the Ajna chakra, and I had a headache and felt slight vibrations. Innumerable purple flowers (with lotus-shaped petals) rotated around my head.

I started experiencing vibrations and rotations in the Anahata chakra, sometimes so heavy that I felt my chest would burst open. All the other chakras rotated.

Another Kundalini Awakening

I experienced one of the most sacred Kundalini awakenings to date, during which I received blessings from Dakini, a Goddess also known as Shakti. She granted me the blessing with the message: "From now on, you will be able to raise your Kundalini whenever you wish. I will guide and assist you whenever you call upon me."

She reappeared after a period and reminded me to share her blessings with Guruji. Following her guidance, I have done so.

Bringing the Holy Padukas Home

A few years ago, I had the vision to buy an Asan (Pedestal, a base on which a statue is placed), Asan cloth (a small square piece of cloth made of cotton, silk, or wool, used during worship), and Padukas. I followed the guidance that I received and bought all three things. Slowly, I began to do pada pooja of Padukas. I had the most magical experiences that one can ever imagine.

Meditation Experiences Post-Initiation

In the initial days of my meditation, I could see gold everywhere: I could see fields of gold, houses, utensils, and roads all made of gold. This continued for almost a month. During this time, I could feel the vibrations and rotations of my chakras. After these experiences, I could see greenery everywhere for a few days.

Once, while meditating, I had the feeling of numbness in my legs and hands, along with a tingling sensation, as if something was crawling all over my body. Another time felt a cold breeze blowing out of nowhere.

There were quite a lot of beautiful experiences during this period, I shared a few that I could recollect.

Gods, Goddesses, and Sages / Saints whom I saw during the initial days of my Meditation

Saw Lord Vishnu sitting on a seven-hooded snake for a few days.

I saw the Gabriel angel blessing me (I have received the blessings of the archangels multiple times since childhood.)

Saw Brahma, Vishnu, and Mahesh (Lord Shiva) all coming one by one in order, giving me blessings, and leaving the same way.

I saw Ardhanarishwar: half Lord Shiva and Maa Parvati through Ajna.

I saw the Lord of Death (Yamraj) on my left. He was waiting to take me with him. I refused. He kept waiting. Just then, Lord Shiva appeared on my right, smiled, blessed me, and said "I WILL BE THERE WHENEVER YOU CALL ME" he took Yamraj forcefully with him in the sky, and left him there, returning to a place full of snow-clad mountains to meditate.

I saw Lord Shiva and Maa Parvati. Maa Parvati was telling Lord Shiva, "Why don't you grant her all the boons and powers? She is so dedicated and meditates on Om so fervently." To this, Lord Shiva smiled and said "Yes, but there is a little more to do." They smiled and left.

I saw Lord Shiva blessing me, and the serpent around his neck came down in front of me happily. I had no fear.

I saw a sage while meditating. His name was shown as Vishwamitra. He smiled and blessed me.

My Meditation Experiences of Different Chakras

While meditating, I saw sunrise and sunset through the Ajna. I could see the sea levels increasing through the Ajna. One day in my meditation, I experienced darkness at the Ajna. Vibrations at the Ajna were intense, and I had a severe headache, which lasted for almost a month. At a point of time, different places could be seen from the Ajna (sea, nature). Another time, I saw an eye and then a tunnel at the Ajna chakra that appeared bluish-indigo. The entrance of the tunnel had white light, which was inviting.

Once, while meditating, I saw many white horses in a meadow. They appeared to be happy and were playing. Another time, in my meditation, I saw all my chakras aligned (like a rainbow). I saw a candle flame at the Ajna.

I saw a divine energy moving up the spine from the Mooladhara. It resembled a white serpent; which reached the

Ajna. The serpent energy, in the form of divine light, could be seen between the two grey lotus-shaped petals at Ajna. From there, it moved up joyfully to the Sahasrara. I saw a lotus opening up completely with innumerable scattered petals. Purple and white flowers were rotating around my head, and the serpent, with its hood raised, was at the back of my head.

I experienced a serpent, in a divine energy form, rising up and going down. This time, it raised its hood and moved straight to the Sahasrara through the Sushumna Nadi. I could feel my body very light.

I saw the Sushumna Nadi as a hollow tube (blue in colour), and the serpent, in a divine energy form, rising and going straight to the Sahasrara. It had rainbow colours on it. After reaching the top, it seemed very happy, protecting me.

While meditating, I started getting vibrations near the Mooladhara Chakra and feeling an energy moving upwards through the Sushumna Nadi. The energy reached the Ajna Chakra, and I had a headache and felt slight vibrations. Innumerable purple flowers (lotus-shaped petals) rotated around my head.

There were vibrations at my Ajna Chakra, the temples, and the back of my head. The heat in my body had increased; I would sweat a lot while meditating and even while self-healing. After meditating, when I rubbed my palms, the heat was intense. After messaging Guruji, the heat problem was solved.

I saw an eye and then a tunnel. The colour appeared bluish-indigo with some lights. I have been seeing this tunnel for few days.

I saw a serpent in a divine energy form, at the Ajna, it reached the Sahasrara and went down. One day, while meditating, I saw a serpent in a divine energy form at the base of the Sushumna Nadi. It was coiled, it raised its hood and went straight to the Sahasrara. I saw a golden star above the Sahasrara. My body felt very light after this experience. I could see nature through the Ajna Chakra for a few days.

Vibration of Every Cell of My Body

One day, after doing an exercise given in our meditation group, I felt heat on the soles of my feet after meditation since morning and was there for a good while. Normally, I wear socks due to the cold climate, but that day I hadn't and wasn't feeling cold at all. I felt pressure on my temples and in my head as divine energy moved from the spine upward and reached the Ajna Chakra. My right thumb vibrated for quite some time. I felt each cell of my body vibrating. It was truly a blissful experience.

First Out-of-Body Experience

Once, while meditating, I saw the tunnel again. My soul entered the tunnel and reached a place where everything was as white as snow. There were clouds everywhere, and it appeared heavenly. I saw a large silvery-white star; my soul passed through it and later came back. After a few days, I saw the tunnel again while meditating.

After a few days, I saw my heart chakra going out of my body at a very high speed. It entered the tunnel and reached space, where I could see planets and stars. It passed by all the planets and then returned.

First Time Experience of Floating Above the Ground

I started receiving a tremendous amount of energy during my daily meditation. I could feel the powerful energies enter my body while meditating. One evening while meditating, I felt my body very light no weight at all, I felt I was floating a little above the ground. I opened my eyes to see whether it was true and could feel some energy trying to keep me afloat. It was just 2 seconds left for my meditation time to complete and I opened my eyes. The experience was very blissful.

Divine Presence, white protective layer experiences

I could feel the holy padukas having infinite energy and also felt DIVINE presence.

In one of my evening meditations, I saw a person in complete white robes (appeared like GOD) blessing me over my head, silvery white protective layer like a cocoon was formed and I was inside it meditating.

Mosquito Bite

Guruji had told us to keep the window little open while meditating. I have faced the situation of mosquitoes biting me, they still do during the whole of rainy and winter season. Early morning there are more mosquitoes. Nothing affected me. During the earlier days after initiation, there would be mosquito bite marks on my face, hands, and legs. More than the bites the buzzing sound near the ear would cause disturbance. I never gave up.

I could meditate in any situation without getting distracted. Sometimes there are many experiences back-to-back, especially on the days when there are kundalini awakenings, as one is in a blissful state, it is difficult to remember all of my experiences, after receiving guidance, I note down the experiences immediately after meditation. Later on, the forgotten experiences may be shown again or if the experiences are in continuation, I remember the earlier ones too and write them too.

First time meditation on a beach and the tests I overcome

In April 2019, after our spiritual retreat, my friend who was coping with her mother's passing and family issues, proposed a two-day Goa trip. I hesitated to leave my Kundalini Meditation routine but agreed. Although my friend struggled to find tickets, her relative, a ticket collector (TC), offered family quota seats on the Mumbai-Goa train.

He arranged to pick us up early, arranged comfortable window seats, and ensured we were treated like VIPs, with attentive service throughout the journey. I kept to my health routine, preparing my green juice onboard while my friend enjoyed the meals. I maintained my meditation schedule and strict diet routine throughout the trip.

One evening at the beach, I meditated under a coconut tree as the sun set, embracing the calmness of my first beach meditation. I began meditating, I felt very peaceful. It was the first time I was meditating on a beach. Within a few minutes something from above started falling on me, it kept falling, I could feel something biting me. I figured out they were insects. Initially, it was a bite, then a few more bites. In meditation, I could see large black ants all over me. I could feel them all over. I was bit on the neck, that one bite was painful. I immediately received an insight; it was happening to distract me. I kept meditating without getting affected. After meditation, I saw myself, there were really large black ants on me, but weren't biting. My friend was shocked looking at me. I dusted them off carefully and checked myself there were no marks and no pain at all. I had got the right guidance.

This experience reminded me that, on any spiritual path, distractions will arise. It's our focus and discipline that guides us through, teaching us patience and calm amidst challenges.

My Chakra Meditation Experiences

After I was initiated into the second level of meditation, which is chakra meditation. I had several experiences on different days during meditation. I experienced Kundalini awakening at various instances.

It deepened my connection to Divine and also brought clarity to my life's purpose. I could now tap my energies that were lying dormant and use them for the benefit of mankind. I gained access to various dimensions of awareness and an in-depth understanding of myself and the world around me.

During my initial days of chakra meditation, I experienced the ability to breathe through all my chakras without using my nose, repeating this phenomenon several times. On another occasion, I saw my internal organs, including nerves and arteries, in vivid detail. I also felt a cool breeze at the entrance of every chakra, followed by a cool sensation enveloping my body, giving me goosebumps. During meditation, I witnessed a stalk with a bud gradually opening at each chakra, blossoming into lotus-like flowers. In one remarkable experience many years ago, I saw a golden and silver star above the Sahasrara, radiating an all-encompassing brightness. I could also see my soul traveling at times and observed myself meditating peacefully on several occasions. At other times, I saw a milky white star above my head that emitted light and energy flowing from the Sahasrara chakra, spreading throughout my body, and I found myself surrounded by a white aura. I witnessed similar visions of a silvery-white star, a golden halo around my head, and even a white dove hovering above with its wings open.

Sometimes later in my meditations, I have experienced unique and repeated visions. I saw a large closed wooden door that slowly opened to reveal a bright white light, its rays reached me. A divine golden light from the Sahasrara chakra enveloped me completely. On another occasion, I saw the hood of a divine serpent near my face, its eye growing larger as it approached, and at times, two grey serpent eyes appeared close to my face, magnifying in size. Breathing through my chakras during meditation often makes me feel connected to nature and its occurrences, while sometimes I even lose the sensation of breathing through my nose. There have been instances where I felt as though ants were biting me all over, especially on my face, accompanied by swaying movements, though no ants were present in reality. On rare occasions, I have also been able to see and hear events moments before they unfolded, enhancing the profound and mystical quality of these meditative experiences.

After a point, due to continuous meditation intense heat had generated in my body. As soon as I sat on my meditation mat, sweat used to drip from my entire body, such that my hair used to get wet. Guruji advised me to stop meditating till my body cooled down and to continue with self-healing. After a few months, the heat in the body subsided and he guided me to begin meditation on alternate days. Later on, he told me to meditate daily but only twice a day.

I released the heat by a specific method and continued my practice. He then told me I could meditate as I used to do (a couple of times) in a day. I followed his guidance.

One evening, a Buddhist monk in an orange robe came and sat beside me. He stayed till the end of my meditation.

One day, while meditating, I first felt myself reducing in size, then increasing in size. I kept meditating. I received an answer as to how it happened.

Once, during my evening meditation, I saw some divine souls in different stages.

I experienced vibrations at the back of my head for a few days.

Since one Thursday, I noticed that my hands and legs would become lifeless after each meditation session throughout the day. Simultaneously, I began receiving an intense flow of energy in the form of white light at the Sahasrara, which spread throughout my body. During these episodes, I was unable to move my hands or legs but could rub them back to normal after a few minutes. Previously, while meditating, my hands and legs would only go numb temporarily, which I would manage by rubbing them. The issue of my hands and legs becoming lifeless was resolved after a few days during an evening meditation. However, the numbness in my legs persisted daily during meditation, occasionally affecting my hands as well. After meditating, while chanting "Gurur Brahma Gurur Vishnu," the numbness would gradually subside and disappear by the third repetition. I could feel the energy moving from my hands and legs to the Mooladhara chakra, where it seemed to be stored, accompanied by intense vibrations that lingered for a few minutes at the Mooladhara chakra.

Receiving energy from Mother Earth

Once again, I felt myself floating above the ground while meditating and felt all my chakras vibrating and rotating. I saw myself receiving white light at the Sahasrara. Interestingly, I started feeling energy under my meditation mat. It felt as if I was receiving energy from Mother Earth.

The Radiance of Kundalini Awakening

Another time, I saw all my chakras in their respective colours rotating. I also felt the vibrations. Two serpents in divine energy form were seen entwined around the Sushumna Nadi. A black serpent in divine energy form rose straight from the Sushumna Nadi to the Ajna and then to the Sahasrara with sparkles of white light all around my head. There was OM written on the black serpent's head

The Protective Hood of the Divine Serpent

While meditating, I saw a serpent in an energy form at the Mooladhara chakra. It was coiled; it raised its hood, and went straight to the Sahasrara chakra through the Sushumna Nadi. Its hood protected me as an open umbrella.

The Mystical Encounter with the Serpent's Eye

Once while meditating, I could see an eye appearing to my right, then to my left, and finally right in front of my face. It was the eye of a serpent in a divine form of energy, which I could identify by the scales around its eye. The eye enlarged and came very close to my face, almost touching it, before disappearing. This was similar to an experience I had a few years ago.

Golden Aura

During one of my evening meditations, there were heavy vibrations at the Mooladhara chakra. All my chakras started vibrating heavily. I could see brightness all around me and I was in a blissful state. Suddenly, there was an energy rush in me. A bright light swiftly passed through the Sushumna Nadi to the Sahasrara, and a pink lotus opened with innumerable petals. There were golden sparkles high up, and everything was golden in colour. I was completely lost in bliss. My aura was gold in colour. Even after opening my eyes after meditation, I could see brightness for sometime and I experienced bliss for a long.

White Light Forming OM and White Aura

While meditating, I saw a bright white light from the Mooladhara passing through the Sushumna Nadi going above the Sahasrara. It formed OM. I saw a bell (it appeared as a Tibetan bell). The bell started ringing; there were sparkles all over. My body was shaking, all my chakras and every part of my body were vibrating. My aura was white. The background was blue.

Blue Aura

One day, while meditating, I could see my aura blue. Simultaneously, I saw the cover page of Guruji's new book that was published later.

Blue and Yellow Aura

For a few days, there were heavy vibrations at the Mooladhara chakra and all chakras, even temples, were having heavy vibrations, on a particular day, while meditating I saw a white serpent, in a divine energy form, moving swiftly through the Sushumna Nadi and going up to the Ajna chakra. My body was filled with white light, which kept pouring from the Sahasrara. A blue Aura formed around me and a yellow Aura formed around the blue Aura. I was encircled in two auras.

Blue Aura

On Thursday, during our group meditation, I saw a pearl bluish in colour at the Sahasrara chakra and then could see the universe. I was guided in meditation that it was a blue pearl. My aura was blue, and I could see blue everywhere.

I saw myself in blue and my Aura deep blue

Towards the end of an evening meditation, I could see myself as an astral form meditating in the cosmos. A purple lotus could be seen spinning slowly above my head at the Sahasrara. A very bright white light from the Mooladhara went straight through the Sushumna Nadi to the Sahasrara. Countless purple lotus petals dispersed and revolved around my head in circles. Within a few seconds, I saw myself and the surroundings deep blue in colour. This was the first time I had seen myself in blue. My aura was deep blue. I was feeling blissful. I have no words to describe the beautiful moment.

White Aura

A few days back, a divine energy in the form of a serpent rose from the Mooladhara chakra, passed through the Sushumna Nadi, and reached the Ajna chakra. After some days, while meditating in the morning, there were vibrations at all my chakras. Ida Nadi, Pingala Nadi, and Sushumna Nadi met at the Ajna, and the serpent in a divine energy form moved from the Ajna to the Sahasrara Chakra. There were vibrations with a very beautiful feeling at the Sahasrara chakra, where a red lotus with innumerable petals opened. It was absolute bliss. I saw two bright golden stars, one just above my head and the other little higher. My aura was white.

New Earth

During one of my morning meditations, I saw myself moving at a very high speed at the Ajna chakra. It was a narrow road through the forests, with greenery everywhere, even at the sides of the narrow road. My soul kept increasing its speed, it reached a block, and there was a huge boulder which blocked the way. I chanted OM NAMAH SHIVAYA, and the block disappeared immediately. I kept going at top speed and reached the end of the road. I was in another world (it seemed as if a new earth was being created). I saw the newly formed forests, birds, insects, monkeys, fruit, and flower-laden trees, the rivers appeared as blue jewels in the forests, saw the seas, they looked amazingly beautiful.

It was a spellbinding experience. I could see the Earth from a much higher point. It appeared bluish in colour, with little white area too as if clouds. I could see all the countries even ours, I then decided to go back and again saw myself moving at a very high speed. I entered through the Ajna Chakra and saw myself on the earth meditating.

Five-Hooded Divine Snake Protecting Like an Umbrella

During a meditation, I got vibrations at the Mooladhara chakra, and all my chakras started vibrating at the same frequency. I then saw a divine snake moving up the Sushumna Nadi playfully. It stayed at the Ajna, and I asked it to move because I had to breathe through the Ajna. However, it was playful and didn't move. So, I tried breathing and could do it easily. Divine snake then went to the Sahasrara and protected my head like an umbrella. It had five heads and was very big. There were showers of flowers falling from above. My aura was white. It was a very beautiful experience.

A Few Teachers' Blessing Me in My Meditation

Once, as I began to chant "Gurur Brahma Gurur Vishnu..." I received energy and felt highly energized. While meditating, I saw a few teachers blessing me.

Ida And Pingala Going Criss Cross in My Meditation

During meditation, there were heavy vibrations and rotations at all my chakras. I saw Ida and Pingala moving from the Mooladhara chakra and going criss cross (spiral movement) around the Sushumna Nadi at my chakras. They stopped at the Ajna chakra. Suddenly, a white light passed through the Sushumna Nadi, Ida and Pingala, went along to the Sahasrara. A white lotus with infinite petals opened, and high up, there were white sparkles all around. The experience was incredibly beautiful.

Bindu Visarga Related Meditation Experiences

Once, I could feel vibrations at the Bindu Visarga for quite some time. One day, I saw some drops falling from the Bindu Visarga to the Swadhisthana chakra.

After many days, I saw some fluid dropping internally from the Bindu Visarga into the back of my mouth. It appeared transparent and milky white, falling very slowly. The drops were being collected in the back (or hollow) of my throat and seemed precious. When I shared this meditation experience with Guruji, during one of our retreats, Guruji's eyes sparkled with happiness, and he happily said, "You have reached the ultimate."

In one of my evening meditations, my mouth gradually started filling with sacred fluid. I could see the precious fluid/Amrut, sweet in taste, dripping drop by drop from the Bindu visarga to the upper palate and collecting in the depth of my throat. I kept swallowing it and felt very energetic after my meditation.

The Dark Passage Under the Mooladhara Chakra

I could see a dark passage directly beneath the Mooladhara chakra, with an energy attempting to pull my soul, though it was unable to succeed. A few months earlier, my soul had traversed the same passage but returned immediately due to the overwhelming presence of negativity.

Higher Loka of Pure Souls

During another experience, I ascended to the higher Lokas, where various stages unfolded. All the souls I encountered there appeared pure, adorned in long, flowing white robes.

High Energy Trying to Push Me Up

Some years ago, for a few days, when I was breathing through my chakras, my breath was going above the Sahasrara in a straight line, passing through some symbols that I could see. I could also feel a strong energy trying to push me up in the air. I had experienced slight levitations twice, earlier, but this time, the energy was stronger. I have reduced my meditation over the past few days.

The energy which was trying to hold me up in the air could not be felt during the next meditation.

My breath started going above the Sahasrara. I was trying to control it, but it was going above the Sahasrara through some symbols.

Chakras Above Sahasrara and Below Mooladhara

Once, during the second-morning meditation, I saw a serpent in a divine energy form, lifting up its head at the Mooladhara chakra and passing through each chakra in a zigzag way and reaching the Ajna chakra. The energy in the form of white light, moved swiftly from the Mooladhara chakra, passed through all my chakras. The movement of energy through the Sushumna Nadi was very smooth. The movement of the serpent, in a divine energy form, could be felt more at the Anahata, Vishuddhi and Ajna chakras. Before this happened, when I was doing the first morning chakra meditation, my breath was going above the Sahasrara and my breath was going below the Mooladhara. It appeared as though there were chakras above the Sahasrara and below the Mooladhara, and my breath was connecting to them from the Sahasrara and the Mooladhara chakras.

After a few days, the breath stopped going above the Sahasrara chakra.

Floating Above the Ground

During one of my evening meditations, I felt myself levitating (floating) a few inches above the ground for a few minutes. I then came down slowly.

Strange Sensation in My Throat

I was having a strange sensation in my throat for many days as if something was continuously moving. While I always have vibrations, this was something different. Later, Lord Krishna guided me about what it was related to.

Asked to Choose Between Two Tassels in My Meditation

During an evening meditation, I started getting heavy vibrations and rotations at all my chakras. I was experiencing vibrations at the Mooladhara chakra over the past few days. I was shown two tassels, they were hanging in front of my eyes, and I was asked to choose fone. I first thought about the colours and felt that yellow represents liveliness and happiness but I decided go with red. As soon as I chose red, a red fluid went up from the Mooladhara chakra through the Sushumna Nadi to the Anahata chakra, and a white fluid came down from the Sahasrara chakra to the Anahata. Both met with great magnitude and proceeded to the Sahasrara, a red lotus with numerous petals opened. I was soaking in bliss.

Folded Hands Doing Pranams During My Meditation

On a Thursday meditation, I saw two large folded hands doing pranams. Soon after, a few more were seen, they were smaller in size compared to the bigger ones. I received a lot of energy and felt energised in meditation. I was in a trance for a few hours after meditation.

Divine Serpent playing and moving happily through Sushumna

Once, for three days, there were heavy vibrations in the Bindu Visarga, Vishuddhi, Ajna and Sahasrara. Generally, all my chakras vibrate during meditation, the top chakras vibrate more intensely. On a specific day, all my chakras started vibrating and rotating at the same speed. I could feel high energy in my body.

I could see two snakes in divine energy form, entwined at the Mooladhara chakra, moving up the Sushumna Nadi. They passed through each chakra on the Sushumna Nadi and waited at the Ajna chakra.

After a while, I saw a divine serpent as white as light. It was small in size, moving its tail happily and was playing on its way up. It went up from the Mooladhara passed through the Sushumna Nadi and met at the Ajna, Divine serpent went up to the Sahasrara. I could see infinite lotus-shaped petals purple in colour rotating around the Sahasrara and my head.

In Cosmos, Seeing Entire Universe

During an evening meditation, I saw a bangle with emeralds at the heart chakra, which turned into a triangle. At the Manipura chakra, I saw a flexible wristband with some stones, turning into a triangle. The whole neck could be seen as completely blue, with a blue stone at the Vishuddhi chakra. At the Swadhisthana chakra, I could see orange gemstones shining. While breathing through my chakras, my breath went up swiftly from the Mooladhara to the Ajna.

I could see a wooden wheel revolving slowly at the Ajna. Soon, its speed increased, and a hollow could be seen at the

Ajna. Suddenly, a huge snake in a divine energy form could be seen; it put its hood up. Almost a month back, the huge serpent in divine energy form had moved happily from the Mooladhara to the Ajna and stayed there.

As I continued my meditation, and as I was taking my breath upwards, the huge serpent in divine energy slid from the Ajna and, along with the breath, moved to the Sahasrara. It had many hoods and from each hood, precious stones kept falling. It was happily showering precious stones all over. A tiara with precious stones of different colours could be seen placed around my head and the serpent was protecting me with its hood wide open. A white diamond could be seen above my head emitting white light. I was in the cosmos. I could see the entire universe.

Another time, as I was meditating while breathing through my chakras, I could see a beautiful blue colour lotus opening its petals at the Vishuddhi chakra. There was a lot of brightness around my chakra. Divine light was glowing throughout my meditation. At the Manipura, I saw shades of peacock feathers on the path (Sushumna Nadi), and the colours split and went to the Sahasrara and Mooladhara. At the Ajna, I saw the cosmos; I could see planets and could feel very heavy rotations. At the Sahasrara and in my head, I could feel vibrations. At the end of meditation before the alarm could ring, a decorated mud pot appeared at the heart chakra, and gold coins could be seen pouring out continuously. A lot of energy flow could be felt at the tip of all the fingers.

Origin of the Ganges River

During one of our Thursday group meditations, I saw the origin of the Ganges River. As the rivulets kept flowing down, the river kept increasing in size. There was a stone bund, that seemed to be broken by the force of the river. I saw two sturdy wooden logs put together (/""""\) in shape. The logs were smeared with orange vermillion colour, exactly the colour of the vermillion used in temples.

On top, in between the logs, there was a brass bell and a cloth tied to its upper part, and below it, there was a Shiva Lingam. The Shiva Lingam had three white lines and a red dot in between the lines. From behind the logs, there was river water flowing. The water kept flowing it appeared as if the Shiva lingam was being cleansed. The background was a snow-clad region with conical trees of various kinds.

Canopy Over My Head

Once, while meditating, I could see a canopy lowering down from the sky and coming towards me. It came and stayed over my head. It was square in shape. Showers of flowers could be seen falling on the canopy and on me. I felt blissful, could relate to it was some kind of an achievement, didn't try to find out the reason, and kept meditating.

DNA Formation on The Sushumna Nadi

While meditating one evening, I saw precious stones in the shape of a flower at all my chakras in their respective colours. It looked very beautiful. My breath kept going through each chakra. Slowly, the gems turned to real gerbera flowers, exactly the same colours of all my chakras. I saw something wriggling and trying to come out from the red gerbera flower at the Mooladhara chakra. On concentrating I saw the tail of a serpent in a divine form. It was red. It swiftly came out and, in a few seconds, passed through all my chakras. There was a DNA formation on the Sushumna Nadi at each chakra, the DNA shape enclosed each chakra. The serpent in a divine form reached the Sahasrara, and a flower shaped like a lily kept pouring white light into me and all over.

Merry-Go-Round Effect with Colourful Droplets

One day, soon after I began to meditate, each chakra vibrated at the same frequency, and I felt divine energy enclosing me. A very powerful aura was created and the energy kept circling me for a few minutes. My heart chakra and Vishuddhi chakra vibrated and rotated at top speed. My heart was pounding. I felt as if it would tear my chest open. My legs became heavy and numb. The energy was too high. I opened my eyes for a second and then closed them again. Instantly, all chakras started vibrating and rotating together.

I saw a bucket at the Mooladhara chakra, a little red-coloured fluid filled it. It moved throughout the Sushumna Nadi and went to the Swadhisthana chakra where a little orange colour fluid got added to it, it continued to the Manipura chakra where yellow colour fluid was added. The bucket kept going up, and at each chakra, the colour representing the chakra kept getting added. Lastly, it went high up the Sahasrara and the bucket turned upside down and the different chakra colours slowly trickled down in the form of water droplets.

It was as if rain fell down from an umbrella or as if a merry-go-round went round. The droplets in each row had a specific colour of the chakra and seemed precious. The colourful droplets kept falling all around me. My entire Sushumna Nadi was illuminated with a bright energy. The sight was beautiful, I was lost in bliss. The numbness and heaviness of my leg soon went away after chanting "Gurur Brahma, Gurur Vishnu…" I felt myself as light as a feather as if some weight was taken away.

Frog Lost in Sadhana, Later Jumped to Enter Center of My Chest

On a Thursday, during our group meditation, I saw a frog with its eyes closed in a forest. It seemed as if it was lost in Sadhana. The trees in the forest looked very lively, the leaves were fresh, clean, and had droplets of water. I could see a very large leaf. As my meditation was getting over, I saw the frog opening its eyes and happily taking a jump towards me. It again took a jump and entered the center of my chest, just then the alarm rang.

The White Light Fountain: A Journey Through the Chakras

On the day of our meditation group's Global Satsang, initially, when I started meditating, I could see the deep blue sky and stars. Soon I could see some planets. Powerful divine blue light energy began to pour in from the universe. It kept pouring at my Sahasrara Chakra and the energy split in two sides and began to form a cocoon around me. I was enclosed in Divine light. My aura was blue.

After a while, I could see Lord Buddha very calmly descending from the universe. He had a gentle, smiling face. He happily blessed me. After a few minutes, my hands and legs started to become numb. After a point, there was no sensation in my hands and legs. I could feel high energy in my body.

Suddenly, heavy energy could be felt at the Mooladhara chakra. It seemed as though an energy shift had happened. The Mooladhara chakra started vibrating and rotating. Within a few seconds, all my chakras started rotating at very high speed, and a white light through the Sushumna Nadi started moving upwards. Another energy, the Ida and Pingala moved swiftly in a DNA pattern. While going up, the white light looked like a musical water fountain. The fountain looked amazing. The white light went above the Sahasrara Chakra and opened up. Each droplet could be seen in white colour falling downwards. There was a lot of brightness all over. The moment was precious.

My Rare Divine Meditation Experience of Samadhi

One evening, while meditating, a Goddess appeared in front of me. She was extremely beautiful. Her aura was powerful, emitting very high energy. The energy around her was like flowing sea waves. She blessed me and disappeared. Immediately, another Goddess took her place. Many Goddesses kept appearing and disappearing one after another. In between, when the Goddesses were appearing, blessing me, and disappearing, I was guided that she is Shakti and has many forms, and I was chosen to be blessed by her on that day.

Lord Ganesh appeared, blessed me, and disappeared in a fraction of a second. Within a few seconds, the partial face of Lord Shiva could be seen. His face was blue. Lord Shiva and Goddess Shakti united. Their union was magnificent. Simultaneously, when their union was happening, I had a rush of energy through the Sushumna Nadi from the Mooladhara chakra. The energy passed through each chakra and reached the Sahasrara. The energy spilled over and everything looked dazzling bright and beautiful. I felt myself complete. Instantly, I could see the blue sky with the full moon shining brightly. The moon's brightness completely shone on me. I could see and feel the universe showering love and blessings upon me. There were celebrations in the upper Lokas. The word ENLIGHTENMENT, in capital letters, could be seen. I was in a state of Samadhi for a very long time. This is one of the rarest divine meditation experiences

I have ever had. It cannot be described in words. I felt grateful to all Divine for their blessings.

Shivalinga at Vishuddhi

Once, while meditating in the evening, I felt an energy at the base of the Sushumna Nadi. Slowly, I could feel some light movements. The feeling was good. Soon, in place of my Sushumna Nadi, I saw a large samai. There were five wicks burning in the lamp brightly at each chakra. The energy kept getting heavier, and I saw a light shooting up through the samai and reaching the Sahasrara chakra.

At the top of the samai, at the Sahasrara Chakra, I saw a formation of OM being formed, with white star sparkles all around. I could see drops falling from the upper part of my throat and getting collected in a semi-circular-shaped organ in my throat pit. The liquid started overflowing. I could see a Shivalinga at the Vishuddhi, and drops of nectar were dripping on the Shivalinga. I could realise the drops were precious and tried to stretch the organ to accumulate the drops. It accumulated every drop, and the organ was full upto the brim. The drops stopped falling. The few drops that fell went straight to the Manipura chakra.

Beam of White Light Forming Serpent in Divine Energy of Form Protecting Me

During one of my evening meditations, I saw a beam of white light entering my Sahasrara Chakra. Soon, the light formed a white serpent in a divine energy form. It had white precious stones on the upper side of its body.

It encircled me thrice and went behind my back, rose up, and stood with its hood open as if it was protecting me. It stayed in the same position for sometime.

A Rotating Crown of White Feathers

During one of my morning meditations, while breathing through my chakras, I saw the hood of a jacket being stitched. Slowly, it opened up as a bowl and slowly got placed at the throat pit. I could then see drops of liquid falling from the upper inner part of the mouth. Drops could be seen collecting. The bowl was full to the brim with pearl-white-coloured liquid. A few drops fell straight to the Manipura chakra and I saw the drops getting burnt. Instantly, a Shivalinga appeared at the Vishuddhi and the drops that were overflowing and falling to the Manipura, fell on the Shivalinga. I could see my tongue in a unique way holding the drops from falling. The overflowing of the precious liquid stopped.

Soon, I saw a jowar crop just one stalk with its bulb or bud ripened. It was placed at the Anahata chakra. It opened up, began spreading the grains, and turned into a chakra, rotating at top speed.

A little above my head, I could see a crown of white feathers rotating. They looked pretty.

A Jyot at Sahasrara

One morning, while meditating, I saw precious drops falling from the Bindu visarga. Soon, two tiny ladders or gates on either side of the throat pit ∧ could be seen. The gates were stopping the fall of drops from the Bindu visarga. As it opened, I could see some drops falling from the Bindu visarga into the throat pit and getting collected. After a while, at the Vishuddhi chakra, I saw a chakra or a disc (like the rings of Saturn) with seven colours of the chakras. The colours were bright and radiant, like the neon colours. I then saw the Anahata, Manipura, Swadhisthana, and Mooladhara chakras in their representative colours. All chakras were bright and lit up (neon). I could see the Ajna white and Sahasrara violet.

Slowly, the Vishuddhi began to rotate. It looked beautiful as the disc was glowing. It rotated at top speed. Tremendous brightness could be seen at the throat pit. I saw Ida Pingala happily crossing each other at each chakra and reaching the Ajna. Just then, a white light shot up from the Mooladhara chakra, passing through the Sushumna Nadi, and reached the Sahasrara Chakra within a second or two. A Jyot or a flame could be seen at the Sahasrara. A white aura formed around me. After this experience, I became blank.

White Light Branched to the Shape of Coconut Branches

While meditating, the flow of breath was very easy. I saw my breath going up through the Sushumna Nadi, passing through each chakra. At the end of my meditation, I saw a soft white light at the Mooladhara. It kept going up till the Sahasrara chakra, branched beautifully in the shape of coconut branches, as if dispersing the light to the earth. The pillar of light that had travelled up returned to the Mooladhara through the Sushumna. This return of the light had occurred only a few times before and was a beautiful experience that no words can explain.

Periwinkle flowers in place my Sushumna Nadi

One morning, while meditating, I saw a row of pink periwinkle flowers in place of my Sushumna Nadi. My breath kept going from each chakra smoothly. I then saw a long stalk of a plant with a closed bud moving up swiftly from the Mooladhara chakra. The stalk moved through the Sushumna Nadi and on reaching the Sahasrara Chakra the bud began to open up. It was a violet lotus flower.

Serpent in Divine Energy Form Blessing me with a pearl

Another interesting experience was when I saw a serpent in divine energy form, rising with a pearl in its mouth and reaching the Ajna, and I saw myself out of my body. The serpent in divine energy form waited at the Ajna chakra till I came back to my body, then dropped the pearl on me, and then went to the Sahasrara. Then I saw a lotus flower with innumerable petals opening in rainbow colours and rotating.

Guruji's Divine Presence

As I added oil to Guru's lamp, I experienced a delightful fragrance that filled the air. It felt truly heavenly as if the fragrance permeated both my nostrils and spread joyfully throughout my entire body, filling every cell with happiness.

Soon after, I sensed Guruji's divine presence vividly. He seemed to bless every corner of my house before disappearing, leaving behind a divine aura that lingered for hours. Guruji later confirmed that he had visited in an astral form.

Divine Miracles During the Lockdown

Flowers Remained Fresh for Almost a Month

Due to the lockdown, no flowers were available, I had an intention to decorate the holy padukas on the foundation day of our meditation group on the 4th of April. Suddenly, a thought came to mind: there were some flowers in the fridge. I checked, and yes, there were. I decorated the padukas in the morning and evening. Later, I tried to recollect when had I bought those flowers as they were still very fresh. The lockdown had started on the 24th of March, the flowers were bought on the 11th of March, almost a month back. I had completely forgotten about them. Although I had bought flowers later, these were safely kept for a purpose.

Everything Delivered at Home at Half the Cost

I was able to have all the juices during the lockdown. Everything was delivered to my home at almost half the cost of what it used to be before the lockdown. I asked the vendor whether he had made a mistake in calculating, and he said "No," this had happened a few times. One day during the lockdown, two of my neighbours from the previous residence had called me, asking how I was managing things as they were unable to get things. I told them, "I called and things get delivered." They couldn't believe it and said that very few shops were open and did not have basic items.

Groceries, Fruits, Vegetables are Dropped to My Doorstep

The lockdown period was the best. I remember that everything from groceries, fruits, and vegetables was dropped at my doorstep without me ordering or paying for them. If I needed something, my doorbell would ring within some time, and the parcel would be left at my doorstep. This still happens.

Once, Guruji guided us in our group, to have Epigamia coconut milk yogurt. Then, without ordering, within no time, a couple of packets of Epigamia unsweetened yogurt along with jaggery, honey, pulses, flowers, and many more items, were delivered to my doorstep at no cost. I never felt short of anything in my entire life. Divine has always provided me for me.

Auto Drivers Doing Pranams to Me

On two different occasions, once before lockdown and once during lockdown, I had taken an auto and requested the driver to wait a few minutes and drop me back. After dropping me back at my building gate, he offered his pranams. This again, repeated. When it happened the first time, I didn't think of it; the second time, I wondered why he did pranams to me. Just after the lockdown, when I went to collect a Book from a member of our meditation group, I asked the cab driver if he could drop me back, as I had to go back within a few minutes. He told me to book it again. I agreed. When I realised I had arrived very early, I told him to carry on, as I didn't want him to waste his time. Soon after I received a copy of the book, the driver called to say he was waiting for me. He had waited for one and a half hours, dropped me back, and refused to take money. I requested him to at least charge the same amount as he had for the forward journey. He then agreed but still took a few rupees less and did pranams to me.

When I shared this with Guruji, he said, "Good. It will happen."

Serving and helping Mother Nature

My First Task Assigned by Mother Nature

I had a wish to do selfless service and help Mother Nature in whatever small way I could.

In November, I was guided to do something good for mankind, 1 could do something good for mankind, and that it would be the first task assigned to me by Nature. Happily, I took up the task and completed it successfully.

I keep helping Mother Nature as and when I am guided, there are several instances, I reveal as much as I am guided to.

Divine Encounters During Retreats

At Hyderabad Retreat

It was my first spiritual retreat with Guruji.

At the Hyderabad retreat, I experienced high energy flow in my body from the very first day, in the meditation hall, and even during meditation. On the second and third day, my eyes kept closing. I could feel some changes taking place in my body. All three days my head remained very hot throughout the day and night. It was my first retreat, and I received healing from Nature instantly. Guruji confirmed I had received healing.

At Kannur Retreat

Water Bottle

I was in the queue for security screening at the Mumbai Airport on the way to Kannur for our spiritual retreat. I had bought the water bottle from a local shop. Right from entering the airport to the flight, no one stopped or questioned me anything about it. Everyone in the queue was asked to drop their water bottles in a tray before proceeding, during security check-in.

When my turn came, the security officer didn't tell me anything. I walked in with the water bottle in my hand and kept it on the table. After checking in, I picked up the bottle. She smiled, said "Thank you," and let me go. I happily collected my bag and proceeded further.

Om Shanti

While having breakfast in Kannur before leaving for Mumbai after our retreat, I realised I had left my printed ticket in my luggage, which was already loaded onto the bus. Despite having the ticket on my mobile and my Aadhaar card with me, there was a network issue at the security check. The security personnel tried unsuccessfully to open the ticket link. They initially informed me that it wouldn't be allowed.

As the second security officer was still attempting to access the link, I chanted "Om Shanti" once. Surprisingly, he suddenly allowed me to pass through, even though the link had not opened. The power of "Om Shanti" is truly remarkable.

At Rishikesh – Online Spiritual Retreat

On the first day of our spiritual retreat, I could feel the Holy padukas warm while cleaning them.

I saw myself at Rishikesh meditating by the banks of the river Ganga. I could see the surroundings, and feel the cold climate. I saw Parmarth Niketan (The structure and name of Paramarth Niketan were shown to me), the river Ganga, and received blessings.

I felt vibrations at the Mooladhara chakra, and all my chakras started vibrating together. I saw my body getting filled with white light. It was very blissful. I then saw a bright white light (energy) moving very fast through the Sushumna Nadi to the Ajna and then Sahasrara. A white lotus opened with infinite petals. The light went up, there were sparkles high up. Everything was pure white and beautiful. I Saw Lord Shiva passing energy from his eyes to mine.

This experience is noted in one of Guruji's books. He gave me his blessings and asked me to share this experience in our meditation group.

My Aura Expanded During Online Retreat

During one of the exercises in our meditation group, all members were asked to cover themselves in white light. As I covered myself in white light, my aura immediately began to expand, covering my building. Within a few seconds, it expanded further and spread up to Bandra; it then continued expanding up to Vashi and Thane. I felt happy.

One day during our online retreat, I felt a very high energy being received at the Sahasrara when chanting the Mahamrityunjaya Mantra. I chant mantras daily.

At Visakhapatnam Retreat

Lord Krishna

I saw Lord Krishna's statue at home. Instantly, I felt his presence around me. He said, "I am always there with you."

A member of our meditation group and I left to be on time for my morning meditation. We were waiting for the lift. It kept going up and down; it didn't stop at our floor.

I told her, "Let's take the stairs, or we may get late." Just then a person somewhat resembling a male member of our group came. Unlike the member, this person was broader, brighter, and had so much glow on his face. He was very swift and walked straight to that member's allotted room and came out within a few seconds, with a pen in his hand.

I asked him if he knew the way out. He smiled and said, "Yes." We followed him. He was swiftly running down the stairs when the last three stairs were left, he disappeared in front of our eyes. Neither she nor I could see him. We both ran and looked everywhere. He was nowhere to be seen. However, we reached on time for meditation.

While meditating I saw Lord Krishna. He said, "I had told you to call out to me in trouble. You didn't, so I came to help you." Lord Krishna continued, "The person you saw was me, and the pen was my flute. I am always with you." He smiled and left.

Guruji was very happy and confirmed that he was indeed Lord Krishna.

Before leaving for the retreat, he had told me, "I will be there with you." I had divine and rare meditation experiences during our retreat. Divine meditation experiences are so blissful and true.

The Cross of Calvary

I saw a large cross while meditating. The sun had set, and the place was getting dark. There was no one around. I was guided that the place was Calvary and the cross was "The Cross of Calvary," on which Christ had died.

The cross appeared old and had some intricate carvings of the letters 'INRI' on it. Slowly, the cross began to disappear, and a dove with open wings could be seen. Then Divine light shone on me. Later that evening, I came to know it was Good Friday. I felt blessed to see it.

Another time while meditating early in the morning, I saw a cross above my head. The cross was special.

Lord Jesus

I saw a huge boulder rolling away. I saw Lord Jesus coming out of the tomb wearing a pure white robe with a cincture or a rope tied around his waist. There was radiance around him. He looked divine. He walked up to me and looked at my name tag (this was a tag distributed to all members of our meditation group during retreats). There was 'Silence' written on that side, on the other side it was written 'Shunya' (Shunya means limitless).

He turned it and said, "You have reached that height. You are Limitless."

He blessed me and left. In the afternoon I happened to check my phone. My aunt and cousin had wished me Happy Easter. Only then I came to know it was Easter Sunday. I had seen the entire journey of Lord Jesus, right from birth, his crucifixion, and resurrection. When I shared this experience with Guruji, he was very happy and blessed me, saying, "Very good. All your experiences are correct"

Just the night before, I had a vision of Lord Jesus. I saw his resurrection. He had worn a white robe. The white aura around him was captivating. He placed his right hand on my head and said, "My dear child, your body, mind, and soul are pure. You see love in everyone and everything. Only when love is pure one can heal others. You can carry on the good work of healing and teaching people to be pure. Your aura now can heal others. When people hate you, it shows their impurity. You keep forgiving them as you always do. I am with you and bless you with abundance."

Lord Buddha

During the silent time in retreat, the organizer asked us to focus on our Ajna Chakra and invite Buddha. Within a second or two, I saw Lord Buddha smiling at the Ajna then Vishuddhi, then Anahata. He happily placed himself at the Anahata chakra in a cross-legged position and remained there for three days The exercise experience was beautiful.

Meditations and Kundalini Awakenings during our spiritual retreat

On all days of our spiritual retreat, I felt a high energy in my body. While meditating, all my chakras were vibrating together. The main chakras such as the Mooladhara, Swadhisthana, Manipura, Anahata, Vishuddhi, and Ajna vibrated and rotated simultaneously. I saw a white light shooting straight like an arrow from the Mooladhara chakra to the Sahasrara Chakra. My body got filled with white light and my aura too was white. There were sparkles high up in the sky. It was truly magical.

I saw tiny glasses half filled with different colours of liquid. The glasses were then automatically placed at the respective chakra locations according to the colours. They formed chakras and looked very beautiful. All my chakras started vibrating and rotating together. I felt as if the cork had opened at the Mooladhara, and high energy was released. I saw an energy passing swiftly through the Sushumna Nadi from the Mooladhara to the Sahasrara. There were colourful sparkles high above. My aura was white. It was true bliss.

Saw COVID-19 Situation Worsening in Advance

Once, after returning from our spiritual retreat, in my meditation, it was revealed to me in advance that the COVID-19 situation would worsen in Mumbai. After two days what I had seen, came true.

Divine Guidance on Aadhaar Card

On the day of my travel to our Visakhapatnam retreat, my cab had arrived, and I was about to leave the house. Just then, some words were softly spoken in my ears. I recognized the voice. It was of Lord Krishna. Though I had carried my paper-based

Aadhaar card, I was guided to carry the other original Aadhaar card (PVC card). The Aadhaar card was shown to me in the locker. I unlocked the cupboard and took the second Aadhaar card along with me. I thanked Lord Krishna as he gave me an insight that my card would get lost, and guided me that it would be best to have an option to travel peacefully.

I left home and reached the airport within no time. The highway was clear. On reaching the airport, at the entrance of the gate near the ticket counter, I saw Guruji and two members of our meditation group. Guruji was very happy to see me early. He hugged me, lifted my bag, and said, "It is light." He then told those two members, "Sruthi aaya, ab sab kam ho jayenga". (Sruthi has come now all work will be done). Saying this, Guruji asked me to join those two members at the ticket counter to drop my luggage.

Guruji himself got my bag tag and said the lady at the counter wasn't accepting the luggage of both those members as the weight was too much. Due to COVID-19 norms, the lady at the counter wasn't ready to combine the weight of their luggage though they were together. Both the members and I went to the counter. One of them gave my ticket to her, she asked for my Aadhaar card, saw it, and told me to place my baggage on the runner. I smiled and told her "We all are together." She smiled back and instantly changed her mind, and told the two members with me, "Okay, you can put your baggage." Guruji was standing far and watching us.

We swiftly dropped our bags and met Guruji. He asked them, "Ho Gaya? (Done?)" We all answered, "Yes, Guruji." He looked at me and said, "Very Good." We all happily proceeded to the cafeteria. Guruji told all of us to have some snacks. We sat at one place. At the cafeteria, I felt I had misplaced my Aadhaar card while putting my ticket back in my bag. I began to check my bag. One member who had checked in luggage with me asked me, "Sruthi, what are you searching for?" I told him, "My Aadhaar card. I can't find it." He told me, "I saw you putting it in your bag. Don't worry; it will be inside your bag." We all had a bite and carried on. Later, he told me to apply for a duplicate. I told him, "Generally if you are on rent, it is not possible to make an Aadhaar card. Somehow my owner permitted me to make one. Making a new one may be difficult. Even if I apply, it will go to the flat where we stayed on rent previously and that we had left. It has been locked since we left. Let's hope for the best." With Divine grace, soon I was gifted a flat and even the thought of applying or losing my Aadhaar card was warded off.

At Mysore retreat

Transformation of Lord Krishna to Lord Vishnu

In the Mysore Retreat, during one of our morning meditation experiences, I saw Lord Krishna. He was dressed in a silk yellow dhoti and had some peacock-designed blue kingly attire worn on the upper half of his body. He had carefully tied his flute with a yellow silk cloth to the left of his waist, he walked about, went up to the place Guruji was sitting, and walked back. He said he was happy senior member talking to me. He had told me to talk to her, and said she has high devotion towards me.

I was meditating and told him, "My breath here is getting disturbed. The energy here isn't good." He came beside me and said, "Breathe; I am there." Immediately, I could easily breathe. Smilingly, he slowly moved backward and gently tried to take a sleeping position on the pool. (Later on, a member and I while walking noticed there was a big pool in the same place that was shown to me). Suddenly a five-hooded serpent appeared, and

I saw the transformation of Lord Krishna to Lord Vishnu. Lord Vishnu blessed me. He was full of smiles. He lay down on the coiled serpent and watched me. I continued meditating.

When I shared this experience with Guruji, his eyes were sparkling with joy, and he told me, "Keep sharing your experiences with me; they all are correct."

Naga Deva

During the retreat, while meditating, I was breathing only through my chakras. The breathing through the nose had stopped. At the Mooladhara chakra, heavy energy, along with a feeling of tickling could be felt. There was a sudden movement, and the energy rose from the Mooladhara chakra, passing through the Sushumna Nadi and all my chakras. Ida and Pingala moved along, crossing each chakra. All my chakras were vibrating and rotating. The energy reached the Ajna chakra, along with Ida and Pingala, and a Trishul could be seen. It moved up to the Sahasrara Chakra, and a white precious stone could be seen emanating pure white light.

After a few minutes, I could see a square stone with a Trishul carved on it. The next day, a member of our meditation group shared a documentary of Kurathiamma Temple. The stone structure, its surroundings, and everything shown in the documentary were exactly the same, that I had seen in my meditation. It was of Naga deva.

Lord Buddha

During the Retreat, there was a meditation exercise to concentrate on our Ajna, Vishuddhi, and Anahata chakras, inviting Lord Buddha. As soon as I thought of Lord Buddha at the Ajna, instantly he was at my Ajna. The same happened at the Vishuddhi. At the Anahata chakra, we were supposed to invite him into our house (heart). When I thought of Lord Buddha, I saw him sitting with his legs folded, meditating.

Currency Notes Soaked in Oil Turn Back to Normal

On Guruji's arrival in the evening in Mysore, while seeking His blessings, a member of our meditation group gave me a glass bottle with some liquid, full upto the brim. I asked her, "What is there in the bottle?" She said, "It is coconut oil for the morning." I thanked her, put it in my side sling bag, and took Guruji's blessings.

Later on, when I opened my bag for the room keys, I noticed oil had spilled. The contents of my bag were soaking in oil. I checked the bottle and lid. The lid was loose. It wasn't closing. Another member of our meditation group, who was there with me on retreat, got worried seeing the mobile, cash, and other articles. She took the mobile from me and began wiping it with tissues. Meanwhile, I washed the bag and cleaned the few items one by one.

She said "Your mobile is gone. It may not work. I am wiping it, still, oil is continuously coming out of the charging socket." I told her, "Don't worry, nothing will happen." There was ₹5,500 cash in the bag. All the notes were soaking in oil. Very carefully, without spoiling any surface of our room, I cleaned everything one by one in the washbasin. Though the phone was soaking in oil it worked perfectly, the only thing was that I had to keep wiping the oil every time. The meditation group member who was with me in the retreat suggested giving the notes to the bank after returning to Mumbai. After coming home, while unpacking, I noticed the notes didn't have even a little bit of oil on them. They were clean and new notes. Before leaving for the retreat, Lord Krishna told me, "Situations will be created so that you will not be able to be with your Guru. You may have to face some obstacles, but nothing will affect you. I am there with you."

Maa Kurathiamma

Almost five years ago, Maa Kurathiamma appeared to me during meditation. Since then, she has appeared to me multiple times in her real form. She is extremely beautiful. I have seen her taking human form. Whenever she wanted me to visit her, my heart chakra instantly would reach her.

Just a day before our meditation group's online meditation, I could see Maa Kurathiamma's Temple and the surroundings. Her words, which she had said to me on a few occasions, could be heard. She had expressed her wish that I visit her, sit in the inner sanctum, and talk to her. My heart chakra was about to leave to visit her. Just then, Maa connected and said, "Wait, don't leave, I am not there." Instantly, I could see a white formation, round in shape and the size of an old 1-rupee coin, coming down from the sky. The formation came in front of me, touched my Ajna Chakra, and went to the Anahata chakra. A small door could be seen at the Anahata chakra. It opened. The energy went to the Anahata and disappeared. I knew it was Maa.

When we went to Kannur for our spiritual retreat, I didn't enter Kurathiamma's Temple, I took darshan from outside as there was a large crowd inside. She had been urging me to visit her. And then, Maa Kurathiamma started appearing to me frequently.

I informed Guruji about this, and he advised me to wait. At that time, due to the high number of COVID-19 cases, Maa Kurathiamma connected with me and said I could see her anytime.

Witnessing Divine Miracles

Significance of Number 11 in My Life

I met Guruji 11 years after my major surgery and was initiated into Kundalini Meditation at 11 a.m. on Thursday, 11/10/2018 by Guruji after 11s years of meeting him. In 2021, Guruji blessed me, saying, "From now on, you can heal any disease." This was 11 years after I met him.

Seeing the flat was at 11 a.m.; The person selling the flat had suggested the time. The flat gift deed was done for me on 11/08/2021 at 11 a.m., the broker selected the time. I shifted to my own house on the morning of 11/10/2021 at exactly 11:11:11 a.m., this timing wasn't planned, it happened naturally.

Many memorable meditation experiences took place on the 11th. For example, I received the blessings and a task to complete from Zeus, who was shown to me as a Greek God. Once, I received a garland of 11 coconuts from Siddhivinayak Temple as blessings. I have just shared a few of those experiences; there are many more.

Feathers at Home from Nowhere

I found feathers in the house, though there was no way they could come in as there was a net. One day, I found one soft feather near the Holy Book, which was kept besides the holy padukas. Feathers still keep coming and are of different shades and colours, even though the windows remain closed.

Shallots Appeared from Nowhere

Once, I had decided to make sambhar. While cutting the vegetables, I realised there were only three very tiny shallots at home, which I had cleaned and kept aside. I didn't want to add regular onions. I left the cutting of vegetables and thought of ordering the shallots before I forgot. Since the network wasn't good in the hall, I went back to the kitchen. To my surprise, there were a few shallots near the cutting board. I was surprised and had a thought, "From where did these shallots come?" I cleaned and kept them aside, and finished cutting the vegetables. The exhaust fan wasn't working, so I took a break, went to the hall, and came back in a few seconds. Again, a few more shallots were there. By then, I had the exact number of shallots required for the sambhar. Instantly, I received guidance on how it happened. The work of Divine could be seen and felt. Throughout my life, whenever I needed anything, small or big, without asking, somehow, I received it.

Dried Drumsticks Turned Fresh

One day, I felt like making sambar and started the process. While cutting the vegetables, I realised the drumsticks were almost dry. I bought them some days back and had forgotten to use them due to some work. I kept them aside and continued cutting the other vegetables. I had a thought, "The taste of the sambhar will be slightly different without the drumsticks, I wish they hadn't dried." Immediately, I received an insight to check the drumsticks. As I turned to see, the drumsticks looked fresh and green. I felt very happy that I could use them. I clicked pictures for memory.

Smiley Balloon

Once, when I opened the window early morning, I noticed a smiley balloon right in front of my window. Within a few seconds, Guruji messaged in our meditation group, "Smile and be happy." The smiley balloon stayed there the whole day till night. The next morning, it disappeared. My day was blissful.

Electric Supply and Water Supply Only in My Flat

Once, the electricity of the whole complex and area had gone, only my flat had electricity. My neighbour aunty rang the bell at 1 a.m. Hesitating, I opened the door. Aunty was shocked to see the dim light on and asked me, "Do you have a backup?" I said, "No."

The next two days, the watchman came early morning to inform me that there would be no water as some tank repairs were to be done. I told him to wait, checked the tap, and told him that the water supply was there. He smiled. There was water throughout the day and night. I realised that only my flat had water when the watchman came again to inform me on the next two days as a reminder. All the neighbours were scolding and asking the watchman when the water supply would be restored.

Positive Change in One of My House Owner

A few years ago, I moved into a rented flat. The owner repeatedly asked me to vacate the flat, citing health reasons. I packed and unpacked a few times as she kept changing her decisions. I came to know she had troubled tenants before me in the same way. She had a habit of not returning money. I wrote to Guruji asking for guidance. He replied, "If anybody tries to trouble you, they only will land in problems. You always be peaceful and not to react to anything." Soon, her health declined, and she stopped troubling me. She began to speak politely and returned my full deposit. She kept in touch after I left the flat and sends me blessings.

Receiving Things That I Hadn't Ordered

I receive things (still do) that I never ordered for. I would call the helpline (and still do) and request them to take the things back. They wouldn't send anyone to pick them up and would often offer me to keep them and sometimes would refund the money. Since it was repeating, I felt it was Mother Nature blessing me. I started accepting them happily as Nature's blessings after informing Guruji about it. This keeps happening regularly.

Bel Leaf

Once on a Monday, as my cooking was almost done, I went to the kitchen to switch off the gas knob of the vegetable that was being cooked. To my surprise, I found a fresh bel leaf lying on the kitchen platform near the gas stove. This was the second time in the past few days, I have found. I was instantly guided to offer it to Gurus lamp. This was the second time in the past few days that I had found a bel leaf in the house from nowhere. I shared the experience and photo with Guruji. He smiled and said, "It is auspicious."

Sweet and Heavenly Aroma

One morning, while adding oil to Gurus lamp, I could sense a sweet fragrance. It was heavenly. The scent swiftly went through both my nostrils, and I could feel it spreading all through my body. Each cell of my body was experiencing joy. There was a feeling of unexplained happiness. The house had a divine aura. The aroma stayed for a few hours.

A Flat was Gifted

Three and a half years ago, a divine soul repeatedly called me up, expressing a desire to gift me a flat. I politely said "No" multiple times. Seeking Guruji's blessings, the divine soul called up again, saying, "Now you cannot say no. Guruji has given me his love and blessings." I said, "If Guruji has given you a go-ahead, I can't say no. Please allow me to seek Guruji's guidance too." When I sought Guruji's guidance, he joyfully gave me his love and blessings.

The divine soul asked me to choose a high-valued property. I politely turned down the offer and said, "Please allow me to see a flat that suits my requirements. I don't need anything more than required." I got a well-done-up flat at a reasonable price.

Eighteen months before the flat was gifted, Lord Shiva had appeared to me and told me, "This flat is too small for you (It was a rental flat). You will need a bigger one." The building, the flat and the interiors were shown to me in advance during meditation. The current flat is selected by divine.

Bel leaf exactly in front of the Ardhanarishwar portrait

One evening, I was guided during my evening meditation to bless the house by sprinkling water blessed by Divine and chanting a mantra simultaneously. The mantra played in my ears. After blessing the house, I went to the kitchen and kept the bowl of holy water.

When I came to the hall, there was a bel leaf lying on the floor exactly in front of the Ardhanarishwar portrait. I was surprised and happy at the same time seeing the bel leaf, as there was nothing on the floor a few seconds back. I was guided to pick it up and keep it carefully. I picked it up and kept it carefully, once again, it was a miracle.

Abundance of Blessings

Early one morning, before leaving for an important task to help the needy, I looked at the Ardhanarishwar portrait and saw a sparkle twinkling on Lord Shiva's face. The portrait is enclosed in glass with a wooden frame. Soon, two more sparkles appeared, looking like tiny twinkling stars. The sparkles kept increasing and spreading, creating a mesmerizing moment. They were blessings in abundance. I captured a video to remember it.

Panchamrut Delivered Free

On the day of the opening ceremony of Lord Rama's temple in Ayodhya, after my meditation early morning, two packs of panchamrut were delivered free, along with the apples and pomegranates that I had ordered.

The Miracles of the Holy Padukas

Holy padukas become warm

One morning, while I was wiping the holy padukas, I felt them to be warm. Since then, I have often experienced the holy padukas being warm.

Holy padukas shift position

I have often seen that the holy padukas shift positions. Initially, when I saw the position of the Holy padukas had shifted a little bit, I wondered, "I stay alone. How could this happen?" My query was answered in some days. The answer I got was unimaginable.... I am guided not to share it.

Flowers offered at Holy padukas remain fresh for a few days

Thursdays are always very special. The flowers offered to the blessed Holy padukas on Thursday remained fresh till a few more days. Many times, I was guided not to remove and replace fresh flowers.

Warm Feet and Divine Presence on Holy padukas

Once in the morning, as I was placing the flowers on Holy padukas, I felt warm feet and divine presence for quite some time. I received an insight to cook food and offer. Soon I finished cooking. After offering my humble offerings, I sat there for a few minutes, then got up to go to the kitchen to clean the utensils.

While passing by, I happened to see a fresh bel leaf and an orange flower near the Gurus lamp. Recently, I was guided in meditation, the lamp is lit for all Gurus. It was a miracle; I had not bought any bel leaves nor had I placed any flowers near Gurus lamp. I was surprised and happy too. I then placed the flower and the bel leaf properly.

I felt blessed to have experienced holy padukas warm. I felt warm holy feet too.

Holy Padukas Glowing While Aartis Were on

One morning, when I switched on the TV, some mantras, which were shown to me in meditation a few months back, began to play. I had earlier searched for the meaning. They were ancient mantras. I was surprised and happy hearing exactly the same words on YouTube.

Soon after that, back-to-back aartis of all gods and Goddesses kept playing like the Ganpati aarti, Maa Durga's aarti, Aigiri Nandini, Lord Krishna's songs, Lord Shiva's songs, and mantras. It went on for more than an hour. I felt good listening to them and could make out Divine was clearing all obstacles and showering blessings upon me. I hadn't heard them ever before.

A divine miracle happened: I had placed a single rose on each Holy Paduka early in the morning. While the aartis were on, I looked at Holy padukas. They were glowing. I had never seen this before, so I went too close to see them. They were really shining.

I Received Warmth from Holy Padukas While Wiping Them

Some days were cold in Mumbai. After a bath early in the morning, I was feeling cold and was wiping holy padukas (Sandals) as part of my daily routine (for Paduka pooja) I felt the Padukas warm while wiping them. The warmth spread to my body, and the chill instantly disappeared. I decorated the Padukas and meditated peacefully, it occurred a few times on the days when it was cold.

Meditation on Sacred Occasions

Mahashivratri Experience

During one morning group meditation, I kept Holy padukas on my lap after wiping them and was putting the Asan cloth, the first time I felt warm Holy Feet and was very happy. Earlier, I could feel the Holy padukas warm.

During meditation, I saw Lord Shiva performing a blissful dance. He was looking Divine. He was happy with my offerings and blessed me. I offered what he had guided me one day prior during meditation to offer: bel leaves and datura fruit.

I went to the market and was guided to an old lady who was selling the bel leaves and datura fruit. I had never seen her before sitting at that place; other vendors usually sit there. She smiled and gave me lots of bel leaves, datura fruit, bel fruit, and lots of flowers. She took only Rs.50/- from me. While walking back, I didn't see any vendor selling the bel leaves or datura fruit.

I offered them at Holy padukas along with some fruits. I offered flowers to Lord Krishna after decorating Holy padukas. He smiled through his statue and I could hear his words, "What about me?". When he said this, I understood that he wanted me to offer some flowers to him, whenever I decorated the Holy padukas. I received a lot of energy while meditating and was in trance for a few hours after meditation, and sat on my meditation mat near Holy padukas for a few hours.

My legs had become numb and heavy after meditation I had to rub them for a long time to get them back to normal. I normally have numbness after meditation almost every day. The numbness goes away while chanting "Guru Brahma Gurur Vishnu…" thrice after my meditation. The numbness of the day before was something different; I experienced it for the first time.

Same evening, while meditating, I saw Lord Shiva collecting a transparent fluid from inside my throat in a very small, rare, tiny orangish vial or glass. He said it was Amrut that was filtered. He held the vial close to my mouth and made me drink the fluid or nectar slowly. He then touched his chest with his hand and applied some ash on my forehead. His body was smeared with ash. He smiled, kept his hand on my head, blessed me, and then left.

Dussehra

On a Dussehra, during evening meditation, I saw honey dripping from the ceiling on the floor, and honey was flowing all over the floor. It appeared as universe was blessing me in the form of honey flowing in my home.

Durgashtami

On a Durgashtami day, during my morning meditation, I saw Kurathiamma Devi coming down in the astral form. While descending, she smilingly blessed me.

Just as she reached the earth, she took on the human form of a village belle dressed in traditional clothes, in traditional jewellery. Her anklets made a tinkling sound as she happily sauntered through the village. I have seen her on a few previous occasions; however, this time, her joy knew no bounds. I felt happy seeing her.

Just Before Rama Navami: Vermicelli pack was shown

Once, while meditating, and even after meditation, many times a pack of vermicelli was shown to me. Later, while I was going through our meditation group videos on YouTube, in between, a sweet dish of pineapple sheera was shown. The recipe ingredients were repeatedly shown to me. I didn't think much of it as I don't have any sweets at all, but I knew there was something to it, which was revealed to me sooner

Ram Navami

One morning, happily after doing pada pooja of holy padukas and decorating them beautifully, while offering flowers to Lord Krishna, he spoke through his idol. I looked at him. With a smile on his face, he wished me, "Happy Rama Navami." I wasn't aware that it was Rama Navami, as I don't have a calendar. I don't buy calendars. I had a thought, "Ram Navami? Maybe it was something related to Lord Rama." I wondered why Lord Krishna was wishing and not Lord Rama.

As I began to meditate, I could see Shirdi and the surroundings. The main temple and Dwarkamai entrance were decorated beautifully with flowers. I saw Saibaba in a white attire, a white cloth tied around his head taking a few steps towards me. He blessed me and entered Dwarkamai.

Within a few seconds, I could see Lord Rama smiling at me. The song "Hare Krishna, Hare Krishna, Krishna Krishna Hare Hare; Hare Rama Hare Rama, Rama Rama Hare Hare" could be heard. Lord Rama blessed me and told me that I could see him whenever I wished. I was shown it was Lord Rama's birthday and was guided to offer some more flowers to Lord Krishna's idol, and that Lord Krishna and Lord Rama are the same but have taken different forms and Lord Rama could take his form when needed in the Krishna idol present at home.

After meditation, when I took the pack of flowers to offer, there were a lot of flowers which I hadn't purchased. I had purchased only one variety and had used the same early morning. I was overwhelmed to see multiple varieties of flowers. While offering the flowers to Lord Krishna, with a very soft voice, he asked me to serve him pineapple sheera. I told him, "I don't have the ingredients, as I don't consume milk, milk products, and sugar."

He guided me to buy it from a restaurant. I picked up my phone to search for a restaurant. Unbelievable but true, there was a number on the screen. I was guided to dial the number. It was of a restaurant that I had never heard or seen. The sweet dish was delivered to my home without any charge. While accepting the parcel I asked the delivery guy for the amount to be paid. He said it was a paid order and ran away. I have had such experiences innumerable times.

Soon, I placed a spoonful of pineapple sheera in the bowl along with a spoon. Lord Krishna very lovingly connected and told me to add a little more. I added a little more.

As I was about to pick the bowl from the kitchen platform and offer it to his idol, he said, "Only one bowl, what about my curd?" From the day he started asking me to offer him curd or Makhan, I have kept a bowl and spoon only for him. He directed me to take one more new bowl and spoon and said henceforth to keep both the bowls and spoons only for him. I placed a little curd in another bowl with a spoon. He told me,

"Add a little more, add the thick chunk of curd." I added the chunk as guided and picked up the bowls to go to the hall. Happily, he asked me to serve him the next day the kheer made with vermicelli. I said, "Okay."

After offering the sheera and curd, when I went back to the kitchen, there was a pack of vermicelli/ seviyan kept on the kitchen platform. I realised it was his doing, and I had to make it the next day. Though I knew Lord Krishna was upto something, now it was clear as to why the vermicelli pack and pineapple sheera were shown to me a day earlier.

Soon, within minutes, wonderful gifts, one after another, began to pour in. These gifts were shown to me in October, and I was told by Lord Krishna to accept everything, without thinking not to say no to anything. The person delivering the gifts would ring the bell, hand it over, or leave it at the doorstep. I never got a chance to ask anything. Before I could ask, the delivery guy would run down.

After sometime, when I went to pick the bowls, a little bit of sheera and chunks of curd were consumed by him. There was only little whey left in the bowl. I had served him thick curd made at home without any whey.

I don't pray for anything. I follow what I am guided in meditation. The universe and Divine are showering their love and blessings upon me.

Nag Panchami

While meditating, I saw Sheshnag, the five-hooded snake, come close to me and cover my head protectively with his open hood. He appeared very happy. He stayed in this position for a long time and then left. It was later in the day that I found out that the festival of Nag Panchami was being celebrated. A friend of mine informed me that it is considered auspicious to receive blessings on this day.

Just Before Janmashtami: Kamadhenu Reached Home

Two days before Janmashtami, I was guided by Lord Krishna to buy a Kamadhenu cow with a calf and place it near his statue on a bed of fresh grass. I came to know about Kamadhenu after visiting Goloka during one of my meditations, where Lord Krishna invited me and gave me a mantra. I had never heard or read about this Loka before that experience.

Despite searching, I could not find a good one according to the guidance I received, so I waited for further insights from Lord Krishna. The next day, just before Janmashtami, at 8 p.m., someone rang the doorbell, handed me a parcel, said it was a prepaid order and quickly left. To my surprise, when I opened the box, I found a cow and calf inside. I was guided that it was the Kamadhenu that had reached home.

The next morning, I decorated the area and offered things that I was told to. Astonishingly, the quantity of grass offered to Kamadhenu would reduce on its own, and sometimes the grass appeared to touch her mouth as if she was eating. I hadn't shared the insights I received about buying a Kamadhenu cow with a calf with anyone. Kamadhenu idol reached home on its own through Divine.

Diwali

On the 1st of November, before Diwali, I had a visitation from Lord Rama in my meditation. Lord Rama told me that he would be visiting me on the auspicious day of Diwali. He went on to add that this time he would be accompanied by his wife Goddess Sita, and his brother Lakshmana, and that Lord Hanuman would follow them. He told me to keep my entire house lit for Diwali and that he may come in from any window of the house.

Lord Krishna had already told me a few days before that I must light up all the windows of the house. I purchased and put up the lights and placed lamps as guided for all windows of all rooms in the house, for the arrival of Lord Rama and his family to my simple, humble home. I felt very moved and equally thrilled by this divine message I received from Lord Rama.

I had just shifted into my home and had yet to unpack and set my home. Due to heavy workload and restricted time and physical energy, I needed more time to set up my home. However, Divine Lord Rama did not pay any heed to my dishevelled surroundings and was happy to visit me and bless me. I can't be grateful enough to Divine for their generosity and blessings.

Next, I saw Lord Krishna as well. I saw the two forms merge. Then Lord Vishnu seemed to appear from behind. I saw him stand up from his supine position, where he was resting on the Sheshnag. He came and stood behind the merged form of Lord Rama and Lord Krishna, and then he too merged with this form. I was shown the true identity of all these great Divine beings. Finally, I saw them all smiling and blessing me.

On the morning of Diwali of that year, which was on a Thursday, I was meditating as usual. I saw lamps lit up at each chakra. All chakras till the Vishuddhi were shown to have brown clay lamps. The Vishuddhi had a blue lamp. The Ajna chakra had a bell, which instantly transformed to a mukut (crown). I understood the indication seeing the bell: Lord Rama had arrived. He was at the door, deciding on the direction from which to enter the house.

At the Sahasrara was a lotus petal-shaped drop in blue colour, which instantly turned to a purple lamp shade in ∧ shape. Next, I saw an X-shaped cross on the mukut. On the upper left arm of the cross, I saw Lord Rama. On the upper right arm was Lord Hanuman. On the lower left arm was Maa Sita, whereas on the lower right arm appeared Lakshmana.

They appeared to be deciding who would come from which entrance. Lord Rama chose to enter the home through the main door. Lord Hanuman split himself into two and came from both, the kitchen and bedroom windows. Sita Maa came from one of the living room windows, while Lakshmana came from the other living room window. They all gathered in front of me where I was meditating.

Lord Rama very softly spoke to me saying, "Ask what you want". I replied, "With my Guruji's Blessings, I have everything I need, if there is any shortcoming within me, you may grant me that blessing." Lord Rama stayed silent.

Maa Sita then blessed me, "May the lamp within you always stay lit." The moment she blessed me, my entire Sushumna Nadi transformed to a large Samai (a lamp that is lit for auspicious events and festivals), having multiple wicks being lit at each chakra.

Then Lakshmana revealed certain subtle truths from the Ramayana. He told me that some people believe that he was unable to protect Sita Maa from being captured by Ravana. However, they have not realised that it was all a divine play and that it was preordained to happen that way. He told me that my purity and devotion to my Guru drew them all the way to my house. He then offered his protection to me.

Next, Lord Hanuman said, "I had visited you earlier and had given a laddu to you. You accepted it but have not yet eaten it.

This time I have brought something else for you." (The precious blessing that Lord Hanuman brought this time, cannot be revealed in the Book)

At this exact moment, Lord Rama interjected, "Hanuman, give it to her." Then, he said, "We should leave now. There must be other Gurus and divine beings waiting to come here to meet her." Saying this, they all left.

Few minutes later, I saw a Devi (Goddess) seated on a lotus, wearing a red saree, and adorned with a lot of gold jewellery. She blessed me with open hands, allowing coins to generously flow through her hands near my feet. The floor was covered with gold coins.

At this time, the lamps that I had previously seen at each chakra, which had been vibrating till now, started appearing as a plate carrying several lamps at its perimeter. Subsequently, energy from my Mooladhara started travelling up in a spiral manner. This manner of spiral movement happens very rarely. On reaching the Sahasrara, the energy passed through the lampshade and spilled over, and countless diyas appeared lit over my Sahasrara. I was in complete rapture over this experience, and the divinity of what had happened consumed me in complete bliss. The house and its aura were very pure and sacred.

Experience Just Before Mahashivratri

As soon as I began meditating, I could see a rosebud, blue in colour, at my Vishuddhi chakra. Slowly, it began to bloom, opened up completely, and rotated at the Vishuddhi. I got a glimpse of Lord Shiva for some seconds.

Lord Shiva was completely blue and had worn a Rudraksha mala around his neck and arms. He had a serpent coiled around his neck. His matted hair, tied up, appeared a bit loose. He was meditating. This time, I saw him in an open place. It seemed as if the snow had been cleared. The ground had reddish-brown mud. The aura of Lord Shiva spread around, and the blue colour reflected on the boundary, which was surrounded by snow-capped mountains. Across the boundary, the mountains had white snow. No one else was around.

After a while, Goddess Lakshmi appeared in front of me. She looked very beautiful and was smiling at me. She seemed very pleased and blessed me.

She had worn a gold crown, a red saree, and lots of ornaments. She was standing on a pink lotus. Slowly, she moved a little and started pouring gold coins from her two hands. The coins kept falling and it formed a circle around me. Soon, she disappeared.

In next evening meditation, I could see Lord Shiva's eyes partially open.

Mahashivratri

Three days before the Mahashivratri, I was guided to stay awake the whole night on Mahashivratri. The timings were shown to me. The entire night, I didn't get a wink of sleep. I decorated Holy padukas and sat with my eyes closed. That day while meditating, I saw Lord Shiva slowly opening his eyes.

He stood up and, in a joyful state, began dancing. His hair, that was tied up, opened, and he kept dancing very gracefully. I had long back seen him perform this dance. On Mahashivratri day, once again, I got to see his mesmerizing performance.

A statue in bronze was shown to me. Later on, after meditation, I remembered during my initial days of meditation, I had seen the same bronze statue. It was then shown to me as Nataraja.

As I thanked Lord Shiva for giving me his Darshan, instantly I felt his warm presence and opened my eyes.

He was live in front of me, smiling and looked magnificent. As he was blessing me, from the left side of his body, an extremely beautiful Goddess emerged.

She was happy and looking at me with lots of love. She had a flawless (Chandan) complexion, and captivating eyes, and had worn a white saree and ornaments made of white flowers. I was shown she is Goddess Parvati. She lovingly blessed me and said, "He (Lord Shiva) is incomplete without me. We are Ardhanarishwar." They took a few steps to the portrait and said their presence would be there in the portrait. (The same portrait of Ardhanarishwar, which I had shared about).

I bowed to them. They both kept their hands on my head and disappeared. I was dazed and couldn't believe what my eyes had seen. Guruji's precious words could be heard in my ears: "All your experiences are correct". It was an unforgettable divine experience. I soaked in bliss.

Sacred Chants and Songs in Meditation

Chant On Dattatreya

Once, I meditated from 11 to 11.30 a.m. All through my meditation, in my ears, I could hear the chanting of:

"Om Shri Gurudev Dattatreya"

I have never heard this chant anywhere before.

Chanting "Om Namah Shivaya" to ward off negativities

During a morning meditation, I felt a piercing pain on my neck. Each second, the pain kept increasing, as if some sharp object was being pierced. I felt this was happening only to disturb my meditation.

I began to chant: "Om Namah Shivaya"

As soon as I said "Om," the pain reduced to half. Before I could complete chanting "Om Namah Shivaya" the pain vanished. I could then feel a cool breeze around me. I continued meditating peacefully.

One day, while meditating, I got goosebumps along with heavy vibrations all over my body and all my chakras as soon as I started chanting:

"Om Namah Shivaya."

I received Lord Shiva's blessings while chanting.

"Mahamrityunjaya Mantra" chant

For a few days, some words were ringing in my ears. it went like this:

"Om Trayambakam Yajamahe,

Sugandhim Pushti Vardhanam,

Urvarukmiva Bandhanan,

Mrutyormokshiya maamritat"

It lasted for a few minutes, and I received a lot of energy and got goosebumps. I had written it down, and now I know the words.

I was guided by Lord Shiva to chant the mantra "Om Trayambakam Yajamahe…" daily, in a specific way to ward off obstacles and negativity. I was shown it's called Mahamrityunjaya mantra. I had forgotten to chant it and was surprised and happy when we had to recite it at our Spiritual Retreat.

Song: Jaise Suraj ki Garmi se…

One day, while meditating, I felt a hand on my head. After a while, I could hear a song. It kept playing repeatedly. As the song stopped, I saw Lord Rama smiling at me. I have received his blessings earlier also.

After meditation, I recollected the first few words of the song and searched for it on YouTube. It was a bhajan dedicated to Lord Ram.

It goes like this: "Jaise Suraj ki Garmi se…"

I heard it many times, as I felt the song was related to my life and how I found peace. I noted the lyrics. As I logged out,

I realised my mobile data was off and YouTube was working without a connection. This was really unbelievable. I felt blessed.

A Song that Was Shown Repeatedly

Some days back, a song was shown to me. The first two lines could be heard. This kept repeating throughout the day for a few days. Since it kept repeating, I heard the complete song and wrote the lyrics. The song touched my heart, as I could relate to every word. After writing and recording the song, the song stopped showing. I got an answer in meditation as to why this song was repeatedly shown.

Karpur Gauram Mantra

Once, a little before 3 a.m., in a vision, this mantra was shown to me in Sanskrit. The background was blue, and a powerful white light was splitting through the blue background. The letters were in white.

I wrote the first few words immediately after getting up and carried on with my daily routine. After that, I didn't try to recollect or think of it. And then, the next morning, the mantra was shown to me in words, and someone was reciting it simultaneously. The mantra goes like this:

Karpur Gauram

Karunaavataaram

Sansar Saaram Bhujagendraharam

Sada Vasantam Hridyaravinde Bhavam Bhavani Sahitam Namami

Guruji was extremely happy to hear about this experience.

Experiences with Divine Beings

Blessings During an Eclipse

Some years ago, on eclipse, I received the blessings of Lahari Mahasaya and many saints who came along, like Sri Yukteshwar, Ved Vyasa, Ramana Maharishi, Paramhansa Yogananda, Adi Shankaracharya, Mahavatar Babaji, Vashistha, many more. Some were Japanese or Chinese too. The names were shown to me while meditating. I don't know any of them, but remembered the names shown and wrote down some of the names after my meditation was over.

Ramakrishna Paramahansa and sage Agastya blessed me

During a Thursday meditation, which we did in our meditation group to enhance the power of Mother Earth, within a few minutes of meditation, I saw a person. His name was shown to me as Ramakrishna Paramahansa. He was in a sitting posture with his legs crossed. He said to me, "Blessings, continue your practice." Instantly, I saw a person who appeared to be a sage. His name was shown to me as Agastya. He was walking towards me, and he looked happy. He said, "Blessings, I am giving you powers, which will be shown to you at the right time."

Mother Teresa

During an evening meditation, I saw Mother Teresa. She was smiling. She said, "You are Nature's chosen child; come help the needy." She blessed me and disappeared.

Swami Vivekananda

While meditating, I saw a person in orange clothes and an orange turban walking towards me. His name was shown to me as Vivekananda. He smiled at me and sat down. As soon as he sat down, I saw another person standing behind him. I was guided that he was Ramakrishna Paramahansa, the Guru of Vivekananda. I received their blessings; they were happy. I had seen Ramakrishna Paramahansa earlier too. This time, I saw him smiling.

Chanakya

During a group meditation, I saw a person with his back turned towards me. He had worn a dhoti and a cloth to cover his upper body. He turned and looked at me. His head was half-shaven. He had a lock of hair at the back of his head, three horizontal lines on his forehead, and a red dot in the center of the lines. I was shown that he was Chanakya. He firmly said to me a few important things that I am not supposed to reveal. He then firmly told me to inform my Guru about his guidance.

Next day morning again I saw Chanakya in meditation. He said, "You can call out to me, and I will give you solutions."

Saptarishis

In a meditation, I saw a few sages coming towards me. Initially, I saw a blurred image; however, as they came closer, I counted seven sages approaching me. They were shown to me as

Saptarishis. Their names were also shown to me. I still have the memories of how they looked. After they had blessed me, they proceeded further.

Agastya

During a morning meditation, I saw sage Agastya. He blessed me while I was chanting "Gurur Brahma, Gurur Vishnu…"

Archangels

During a morning meditation, a few archangels appeared. Their names were shown to me, and I recognized one of them immediately. They were archangels Saint Michael (the protector), Saint Gabriel (the revealer), Saint Raphael (the healing archangel, the one who heals the soul and grants grace and purity), Uriel (angel of wisdom and truth), Camael (angel of strength) and a few more. I had received Saint Michael's blessings a few years back in meditation, and I had seen him when I was a kid. Later someone wished me a happy feast of Archangels, till then I wasn't aware of the feast. It was lovely to receive their blessings on a day dedicated to them.

Naga Sadhu

Once, in meditation, I saw a sadhu in the snow-clad mountains with long matted hair tied up high. He had ash smeared all over his body, and beads around his neck. His face was slightly facing upwards. He was sitting in a lotus pose with half eyes open. Through his eyes, high energy could be seen going out to the universe. The word "Naga" was shown to me.

After a second or two, from the half-open eyes of the Naga Sadhu, two Jyot or flames came out floating towards me. The Jyot or flames went into my heart. I got a jolt and felt a sudden energy increase in my body. Soon, the Naga sadhu disappeared.

Mahavatar Babaji

While meditating, I received the darshan of Mahavatar Babaji. His name was shown to me. He said, "I am very pleased with your devotion to your Guru. I will be pleased if you accept to be my disciple. I will come in an astral form to guide you."

I told Him, "I have a Guru."

He said, "I will wait for you to say yes." blessed me and disappeared.

I noted his description and later on, shared it with Guruji. Guruji had told me you will keep receiving blessings of higher beings, note their descriptions and all your meditation experiences immediately after your meditation, and send them to me.

Shri Shirdi Sai Baba

During a group meditation, I saw a sketch. It had an oval face outline, and at the side of it, it had a cloth outline. Greyish-black stone walls could be seen in the background. Slowly, an image could be seen, and I could see Sai Baba smiling at me and saying, "Sabka Malik Ek." Saibaba blessed me.

From his right hand, divine light kept coming to me. The image then disappeared. After meditation, I could recollect that they were the same walls of Dwarkamai in Shirdi.

Parasnath God

I feel blessed to have received the blessings of Parasnath God one morning in a vision. I haven't read or heard about him before.

Lord Shani

One Saturday, while meditating, I could see a person riding a chariot in a hurry, coming towards me. He stopped in front of me, got down from the chariot, and stood near me. I was shown that he is Shani.

He was dressed in a kingly attire and had worn a crown, long heavy gold neck pieces, gold amulets, solid triangular bracelets, anklets on his feet, a pure white dhoti, and a cloth across his shoulder. It appeared as silk material. There was gold work on the borders of the whole outfit. He had some weapons in his hands, such as an axe, a bow, and arrows.

He stood smiling, blessed me with prosperity, and left in his chariot. After meditation, I recollected the face of an old man that I had met in Shani Shingnapur many years ago. The old man's face, height, body, and complexion were exactly the same as Lord Shani, whom I saw in meditation.

Late evening, I came to know through someone it was Shani Amavasya, it is considered auspicious and related to Shani Dev. She went on. I told her I knew nothing about it. I felt happy as I had received his blessings in the morning.

Lord Dattatreya

As I began meditating, Lord Dattatreya appeared in front of me. I was shown that he is called Lord Dattatreya (Lord Datta). I had seen him earlier in meditation. And then, instantly, I saw Lord Brahma, Lord Vishnu, and Lord Mahesh.

I was guided that Lord Datta, and Lord Brahma, Lord Vishnu, Lord Mahesh are the same. I had seen Brahma, Vishnu, and Mahesh during my initial days of meditation, a couple of times, and had even received their blessings.

Lord Datta's figure had three heads, and six hands holding symbolic articles like a Shankh (conch shell), a chakra (wheel), a japmala (a string of holy beads similar to a rosary), a kamandal (water pot), a small drum, and a trishul(trident). He was wearing a garland of fresh flowers around his neck and arms, a Rudraksha mala, and he had his hair tied up. He had worn a light-yellow dhoti.

There was a white small cow and four dogs right behind him. In a few seconds, I could see him holding a large glass of milk filled up to the brim.

He offered it to me and said, "Have it." I told him, "As advised by my Guruji, I don't drink milk or consume milk products."

He told me, "Have it. It is to remove the negativity that has come to you from other people".

I began thinking what to do. That's when he said, "Don't worry, the milk is from the cow named Kamadhenu, who is always with me. I will not guide you wrongly."

He then smiled and said, "You are not drinking it in real, so you will not be disobeying your Guru."

I took the glass from him and drank the milk. Just then, I could see Swami Samarth smiling at me and disappearing (His name was shown to me; I didn't know anything about him or Lord Datta till then).

When I was almost finishing the milk, I could also see Lord Hanuman. He was resting, lying sideways, smiling, and looking at me drinking the milk. Instantly, I remembered him telling me that I hadn't eaten the laddu that he had given me long back. I recollected the place where I had kept the laddu and picked it up.

After finishing the milk, I gave the glass back to Lord Datta. He was very happy, blessed me, and disappeared. I then ate the laddu given by Hanuman.

Then Lord Hanuman said, "I am happy you ate it. I can now get something else for you." Saying this he too vanished. I continued meditating.

God – The Father

One day, in a vision, I saw an old man with his arms wide open, smiling and coming down through the clouds and white rays shone on me. The place became too bright.

He had worn a loose, flowy white robe, and had a silver-grey beard and hair. His hair was long, reaching a little below his shoulders. I was trying to recognize who he was, and I was shown he is God, The Father.

He came close and floated a little above me, and placed his right hand above my head. Instantly, there was a shower of white flowers on me. Slowly, the flowers stopped falling, and it became dark, and God, The Father disappeared. I woke up and checked the time. It was 2:45 a.m. Just then, my alarm rang, and my day began.

I called a priest known to me and told him what I had seen in my vision. The priest told me, "In Christianity, we have the father, son, and the Holy Spirit. You had earlier shared with me about receiving the blessings of the Lord Jesus and the Holy Spirit; today, you have received the blessings of God, The Father. He is considered the Almighty God, creator of heaven, and he is the highest in Christianity. I am noting your visions, meditation experiences, and miracles. Pleased to know, your experiences are manifesting in real life. Hope to see you soon. I want to hear more from you."

My Astral Travel Experiences

Naga Loka or The Snake Kingdom

During one of my evening meditations in 2020, I saw a place which appeared like the entrance of a National Park or forest, with rare trees. It was inviting me. It was misty due to rains, and there was no one to be seen. I was guided to enter, and I did. After going a little ahead, I saw two huge snakes with their raised hoods touching each other. There was a gap formed, I walked through and kept going, it seemed an uphill climb task, very mystical at a point. In front of me, there was darkness and no way. I turned back, and that too was blocked. Above me also got blocked, and I was trapped. I immediately sat down without fear and started meditating. A path could be seen I passed through it, went ahead as guided by a very old snake, and then reached an entrance.

I stood at the entrance and saw a huge snake kingdom they appeared good to me. I saw them all peaceful, happy, and relaxing. Their kingdom was magnificent. There was a huge snake with seven hoods, and there were innumerable snakes of different shapes, sizes, and colours, including golden snakes. They all looked magnificent.

I was contented seeing it. It was difficult to reach; I was tested but cleared the hurdles with ease. They saw me but didn't try to harm me. They were happy with my presence.

Vaikuntha

Once, I saw myself in the cosmos. I saw Lord Vishnu lying on a five-hooded snake in the cosmic ocean. The snake's name was shown as Sheshnag. Lord Vishnu seemed happy.

Seeing me, he got up from there, walked up to me, smiled, and said, "Now you have come. We were waiting for you, so you will be on earth and here." I did pranams and entered Lord Vishnu's abode. It was shown to me as Vaikuntha. I could see Lord Krishna resting.

Deva Loka

While chanting "Gurur Brahma Gurur Vishnu...," on a Thursday meditation, I could see many Gurus and Gods. Among them, I saw someone who directly was looking at me. He was walking behind the Gods that I could see.

As soon as I started meditating, I saw someone coming down through the clouds. He was the same one who was looking at me, dressed in a white dhoti. His hair was tied up in a bun with flowers around it. There was a flower garland and a Rudraksha mala around his neck, as well as Rudraksha beads tied around both his arms and flowers on both his wrists. He had carried a musical instrument, veena in one hand and a wooden clapper in the other hand. I was shown that he is Narada and that he could travel anywhere.

He came clapping the wooden clapper and said "Narayan Narayan. Dev Loka se Sandesh hai Tumhare liye. Tumhare Sadhana se devlok ke Devi, devta prasann hai. Tum apni Sadhana Karo aur shigrah, Dev Lok laut Aao. Narayan Narayan." (There is a message from Dev Loka for you- The Gods and Goddesses of Dev Loka are pleased with your devotion. Continue your meditation and return to Dev Loka soon. Narayan, Narayan). Saying this, while clapping his wooden clapper, he went away.

I could see a place; it appeared as heaven. I was shown that it is Deva Loka. I could see many Gods and beautiful Goddesses. They all looked divine, very happy, and peaceful.

Swarga Loka

I saw myself in Swarga Loka; the name was shown to me. I saw a white elephant at the gate. I was shown that it belonged to Lord Indra. The gate was rust-coloured having intricate designs made of gold. I saw beautiful women dressed up, and I was shown that they were apsaras. I saw very rare flying vehicles with gods and Goddesses seated in them. I saw Lord Indra. Everything appeared heavenly. All were very, very peaceful and greeted one another with love and respect.

Brahma Loka

In one of the group meditations, to create powerful positive energy around the globe, as soon as I began chanting "Gurur Brahma Gurur Vishnu…," I felt someone above my head. I could see Lord Brahma. I recognised him as I had received his blessings during my initial days of meditation. Just a little above my head, I saw him smiling and looking at me. He sent blessings.

He had worn crowns on all his heads, had a white beard, and had four hands holding different articles like a book, a japmala, a lotus, and a pitcher. He was sitting on a lotus and had a white swan next to him.

As soon as I started meditating, I could see my aura expanding very fast. It was white in colour. I could see that my energy was powerful and it was going around the globe. The

Earth was absorbing the energy. I kept sending energy. After a while, I could see a few hands coming out of the globe, asking for help. I sent energy to each hand that I could see, one by one, very swiftly. Slowly, all the hands went inside the globe.

I saw Lord Brahma smiling at me. He invited me to Brahma Loka. I then saw my soul going at top speed through the Ajna. The passage was pitch dark. I reached a place full of lotus flowers. I could see myself amidst nature, swinging on a swing made of branches of trees and lotus flowers. There were lotus flowers everywhere. I was shown that it was Brahma Loka.

I was very happy. After a while, I came back and continued meditating, and tried sending energy around the globe. Just then, the alarm rang. I tried sending energy after the alarm rang but couldn't. I was shown that we were given a specific time to send energy, and the time was over.

Lord Brahma was there till I completed my meditation. While chanting "Gurur Brahma Gurur Vishnu…" thrice, Lord Brahma was smiling at me. He said, "You're welcome anytime to Brahma Loka." He blessed me again and disappeared.

When I had been to Vaikuntha, I was shown that I would visit Satya Loka soon. I felt very peaceful and happy after meditation; the whole day was blissful.

Birth Place of Jesus

During a morning meditation, I saw Jerusalem, Bethlehem, Nazareth, Galilee, Calvary and Golgotha. The streets were cobbled, and the city looked ancient. I went to a place named the Church of Sculpture.

I saw Jesus's birthplace, the place where he walked among the people with the cross before being crucified. I saw the place of crucifixion the tree used for making the cross on which he was crucified. I saw the tomb where he was laid to rest after he died on the cross. There was a mystery in that place. I saw Mount Sinai. I saw the place where Jesus's father used to work as a carpenter. I saw a huge stone wall where people pray.

Pyramids of Egypt

During an evening meditation, I saw the pyramids of Egypt and the Sphinx. I went to the base of the pyramids and saw many mummies. I came out and observed the structure of the pyramids. I could feel that high energies had kept the pyramids intact.

Mansarovar Lake

Once, I saw myself meditating at the shore of a lake. The name shown to me was Mansarovar Lake. The lake looked marvellous. The water was crystal blue, some energies could be seen and felt.

I have been there twice in meditation. Once, I saw myself there on a no-moon night. I saw a few bright lights resembling shooting stars swiftly entering the lake. High energies could be felt.

Siddhivinayak

On a Thursday evening, after meditating for a while, I could see a sparkling floor, and soon I saw many people gathered. It seemed like a temple. The closed doors of the inner sanctum opened, and I could see Siddhivinayak Ganpati.

Almost a month ago, in meditation, Lord Ganesh had appeared and asked me to visit him. A few days back, I was again reminded to visit the temple. It was revealed to me that Lord Ganesh is also called Vighnaharta and that he was always there with me, clearing the obstacles of my life. I was shown that he will continue to remove the blocks that come my way. The word Vignaharta was shown to me.

Gurudwara

In an evening meditation, I could see myself entering the Golden Temple premises in Amritsar. I went inside the Gurudwara and went straight to the canopy where the Guru Granth Sahib is kept. I picked it up, held it in my hands for a few seconds, kept it back, and left. There is a lake surrounding the Gurudwara, a pathway to reach the Gurudwara, and a place to wash our feet. My soul, after visiting, happily came back.

Pashupatinath Temple

In one of my evening meditations, I saw the Pashupatinath temple in Nepal.

Higher Loka and Huge Jaw

During one of our group meditations, while meditating, I saw a huge open jaw. The jaw appeared square in shape and was pink in colour. Innumerable teeth of different shapes and sizes could be seen. It didn't look good but was inviting. My heart chakra went out at high speed and entered the jaw. It seemed like a large tunnel, my heart chakra kept going through the path at top speed. There was a little bit of light. Slowly, brightness could be seen.

As I was almost reaching the end, there seemed to be bright, dazzling light. I merged with the white light energy. It appeared as if I was in some higher Loka. I was in another world. The energy there was high and positive. It engulfed me, and it kept entering me. I was enjoying the blissful moments. After a while, my soul decided to leave as the light still kept pouring into me from all over. My soul swiftly came back and entered the heart chakra.

Snakes Leaving the Earth to Another Loka

One evening, as I began my meditation by chanting "Gurur Brahma Gurur Vishnu…," I could see a dark secluded forest. A bright full moon could be seen. That was the only source of light in the dense forest. I could see countless snakes entangled in a pattern, going up in the sky to a far-off plane. I could make out, they needed help. Instantly, I received an insight, that they were troubled and, hence chose to leave the earth. Chanting, I tried to find the source from where the serpents were leaving. I could see a heavy stone lid move and the fire was ablaze, inside. I could see the last batch of entwined serpents going towards the sky. I stopped chanting and began meditating. I was shown a Loka where they were heading.

Char Dham

On a Thursday, during our group meditation, as I began meditating, my heart chakra went out, reached our meditation group's centre, and came back.

Soon, I saw some temples in four different directions: East, West, North and South. The temples were of Jagannath, Dwarka, Rameshwaram, and Badrinath. I could see the deities. I was shown it is Char Dham. I had never heard about Char Dham.

Many Gods appeared together in a group and blessed me. A mantra kept playing, and the breath through each chakra kept going very smoothly. Towards the end of my meditation, I saw a bright, powerful energy coming towards me. The energy reduced in size and speed, entered through my Ajna Chakra and spread to all the parts of my body right upto the fingertips. I had a Kundalini awakening.

Holy Places in my meditation

Once, while meditating in the morning, some places were shown to me: Kashi or Benares, the Ganga Aarti, Vishwa temple, and all the ghats. It was a blissful experience.

Holy Place where Mahavatar Babaji stayed and Meditated

During an evening meditation, Mahavatar Babaji appeared and blessed me. He wanted me to join him and requested the same. My heart chakra agreed to travel with him. Babaji took me along with him to a far-off place full of snow. I could see a few people, but no one could see us.

He told me, "I wanted you to see the cave where I stayed and meditated." He took me to a place which appeared as a cave. There were some steps before reaching the cave. At the entrance of the cave, there was a brownish-red coloured metal door with iron rods.

As we reached the entrance of the cave, the lock on the door automatically opened, and the door opened too. He told me, "This is my humble place." There were some rugs placed on the floor. He revealed that he doesn't have a body but can anytime take any form if he wished.

He said some people can see him if he wishes, but they won't be able to recognize him. He has met a few of them in his real form. He was very happy as I visited his place. Soon, he brought me back and left.

Dwarka

One day, I took rest for sometime. I rested at 3.40 p.m. At 4.20 p.m., my eyes opened. I was guided to meditate at 4.44 p.m. While meditating, the breath was smoothly passing through the channel and chakras. It was a beautiful feeling.

I could see a huge five-hooded black serpent, coiled and made of black stone, resting in deep waters. Its hood was raised, and milk was being poured in the water. The milk kept pouring on the hood of the serpent.

I could see a city that had been submerged underwater and was shown it is Dwarka. The city appeared ancient and had many beautiful palaces with pillars, intimate carvings, pottery, and precious stones. The palaces had precious jewels.

I could later see multiple galaxies, one after the other. The colours were soothing to the eyes. It seemed as though there was a dance of galaxies. The swift moments looked mesmerizing. The colours encircled me and I was shown that I was Nature.

At Lumbini with Lord Buddha

In a morning meditation, the day before Buddha Poornima, Lord Buddha came and took me along to his birthplace, Lumbini. He showed me a part of his past life, in short, his journey, and the places that he travelled. He told me of whom he was an incarnation. He blessed me with a boon: I would be able to bless a childless couple with a child. Earlier, he had blessed me with two powers (siddhis) and a treasure of blessing, which I am not allowed to share. All of my experiences with Lord Buddha are holy and exceptional. I have no words to thank Divine for their grace and blessings.

Mount Mary Church

One evening, towards the end of my meditation, I was shown a part of Mumbai. Mount Mary church and its surroundings could be seen. It looked beautiful with lights.

Another time, while meditating, I saw Mother Mary ascending and pouring divine light at my Sahasrara. I was covered in it. Instantly, I saw myself in Bandra Mount Mary Church. The statue turned live, she walked down to me, kissed my hands and forehead, blessed me, and disappeared, and was again in a statue form.

Kamakhya Devi's Temple

While meditating, I saw a stone temple and its surroundings. The temple looked very old and was made of black stone. My soul instantly left and reached the temple. As I entered the inner sanctum, I could see a Goddess in real form radiating energy. There was no idol, but female genitals could be seen carved in black stone. And some red liquid could be seen flowing from the genitals. It appeared as blood. Despite all this, there was something very sacred about this place.

The temple followed strange rituals. It was shown to me that it was the Kamakhya temple. I was guided that this temple is a Shaktipeeth. I was also guided not to reveal the entire experience. On this day, there were a few experiences back-to-back. Almost an year ago, I had twice visited this temple in an astral form.

On one occasion, Goddess Kamakhya wanted me to visit her. Since I had earlier seen the strange rituals, my soul was hesitant to go there again. Goddess Kamakhya instantly appeared, stretched out her hand, and asked me to hold it. I held her hand. She took me along with her to the Kamakhya temple, put a garland of flowers around my neck, and bestowed me with some powers. She then brought me back and slowly disappeared. It is a rare and magnificent experience that I briefly share as I am guided.

Lady of Vailankanni

While meditating in the evening, I could see my soul going out of my body. My soul seemed like a white apparition with a silver cord attached. It kept going along a lonely road amidst the forest. The speed of my soul kept increasing. Suddenly, from the sides of the narrow road, dry leaves and shrubs began to gather along the entire path. They kept collecting and moving at top speed ahead of me.

My soul fearlessly kept going at a high speed. The entire collection of leaves and shrubs suddenly moved away from the narrow path to the right side of the road. Something could be seen forming. My soul went and waited in front of the huge formation that was almost the height of three floors. Slowly, our lady of Vailankanni could be seen, with a golden halo around her. She appeared very happy and blessed me with good health and healing powers to heal anyone.

Encounters with Lord Vishnu and His Avatars

Lord Vishnu Blessing Me in His Various Forms

I have received the blessings of Lord Vishnu in various forms like Narasimha, Parshuram, Vamana, Varaha, Matsya, Rama, Vitthal, Krishna, and Kurma (tortoise form of Lord Vishnu).

Lord Vishnu seated on a five-hooded large snake

During an evening meditation, while doing my chakra meditation, I was breathing through a channel. As I was breathing upwards, I could feel and see something huge and heavy trying to come out of the water. The blue water appeared as the cosmic ocean. I saw Lord Vishnu coming out, seated on a five-hooded huge snake. He was smiling and blessed me.

Lord Balaji

During a meditation, I saw an energy resembling a cloud bluish-white in colour, above my head. Energy in the form of white light kept pouring at the Sahasrara.

After a while, I saw a God appearing. He was in front, very close to me. The name shown to me was Venkateshwara or Balaji. He had a dark complexion and a white tilak in a U formation on his forehead. He had worn lots of flower garlands. White divine light from his eyes kept coming to me. He gave me blessings and disappeared. I had seen him earlier too; this time I received his blessings.

Lord Narasimha

While meditating, Lord Narasimha appeared before me. Very heavy energy could be felt next to me. When he appeared, there was too much brightness all around. I was shown that he was Narsimha, the avatar of Lord Vishnu.

The top half of his body was of a lion and the lower half was of a man. His aura was very, very powerful.

He blessed me and said, "No one will be able to harm you". He kept his right hand on my head, encircled me in his aura, stayed for a few seconds, and then disappeared. I was dazed but continued meditating.

Varaha

In an evening meditation, I could see the blue sea. Slowly, from beneath the sea, I could see the face of a boar rising up through the blue waters, carrying the earth on his tusks. As he rose, I could see that he was half animal and half man.

He had worn a gold crown and gold ornaments. He had four hands. Each hand had held something: conch, gada or mace, a chakra, and a lotus. He seemed to be some God and looked very strong. The upper part of his body had ornaments; on the lower half of his body, he wore a silk dhoti orange in colour.

He blessed me, and while he was blessing me the name VARAHA was shown to me in capital letters. He said, "Bhu Devi has also blessed you." He indicated that the Earth is called Bhu Devi.

At that very moment, I could see a beautiful, smiling Goddess with long hair sitting on the Earth. She had her feet placed on a large lotus. Slowly, they both disappeared.

Never have I heard the names of the Gods or Goddesses, nor have I seen their pictures.

Lord Vishnu granted my wish

One morning, while meditating, I saw a potter's wheel spinning next to me. Soon, a God appeared. He was standing in the place where the potter's wheel was. I was shown he was Lord Vishnu; I recognised him immediately, as I had seen him earlier and in Vaikuntha.

He was blue in colour. He had worn a gold crown and a necklace with a precious jewel at the chest. He had also worn gold ornaments like earrings, necklaces, armlets, bracelets, and garments yellow in colour. He had a U-shaped tilak on his forehead, similar to Lord Krishna's and a vertical line in between. He had four hands, each holding different articles: a wheel on his upper right hand which was spinning slowly, the other hands held a conch shell, a lotus, and a mace. He stood smiling and asked me, "What do you want?"

I said, "I want people to be peaceful and happy," without expressing how everything had come to a standstill. I could feel him reading my mind. I also requested him to take away the health problems if there were any.

He said, "Your wish will be granted." He then left. After Lord Vishnu left, I could not see the potter's wheel, it had disappeared. Soon, Corona was eradicated from the earth.

Visiting a New Planet

Guided by Lord Vishnu, I visited a planet. When I reached Vaikuntha, he directed me to see the new planet. After my visit, Lord Vishnu, with a smile on his face, happily told me, "It's new." Then, he blessed me.

The next day, my cousin sent me a news article with some images. The write-up was about scientists declaring the existence of more planets like Earth. I was overwhelmed seeing the pictures and reading the article, as I had visited those planets. The images 100% matched the description I had noted one day prior.

Lord Vishnu In His Matsya Avatar

I received the blessings of Lord Vishnu in the Matsya avatar. How, why, and in which yuga, he incarnated in the Matsya avatar was shown to me, although I had never heard or read anything about the same before.

I could see a half-fish and half-man rise from the waters, and I received his blessings. Earlier, too, I had seen and received his blessings in this form.

I was shown he was the Matsya avatar, one of the first incarnations of Lord Vishnu during Satya yuga. After he gave me his blessings, why he took this form and many more things were revealed to me.

Shri Hari Vitthal

In one meditation, I saw Shri Hari Vitthal. I wondered why he was named so. I had seen him earlier in meditation and wondered why he was named Vitthal. In response to my unspoken question, my attention was drawn to the brick, or veet (in Marathi, the language of Maharashtra, where he has the most devotees following) he was standing on. His name, Vitthal, comes from this veet or brick.

I noted their descriptions and shared them with my Guru. He blessed me.

Divine Encounters with Lord Jesus

Lord Jesus Smiling at me

On one Wednesday, during meditation, I saw Lord Jesus. His face was emitting divine light, and he was happily smiling at me. I also saw a golden chalice near him.

Another world with a cave-like entrance

One day, during meditation, I saw a cave-like entrance at the Ajna. My soul went through it and reached another world. It looked beautiful. I saw Lord Jesus, who looked radiant. He was very happy to see me. I received his blessings and came back happily.

Lord Jesus says, "Heaven welcomes you anytime"

I saw Jerusalem city, all the streets, and the stable where Lord Jesus was born. I saw Lord Jesus standing next to me. He was dressed in white robes and had a pleated cloth belt around his waist. He said, "You have seen my whole life on earth. You are not an ordinary person. You have come on earth to lessen the sins of the world. You took suffering in human form; heaven welcomes you anytime." I could see a gold halo above my head, and when I looked up, I could see heaven. He blessed me and disappeared.

Lord Jesus as shepherd

During a meditation, I saw Lord Jesus dressed as a shepherd. There were lambs next to him. He blessed me.

Lord Jesus said he was and is always there with me

I have had multiple divine experiences with the Lord Jesus. Once, in December, I had a wonderful meditation experience with Lord Jesus. He explained something on healing that touched me a lot. He asked me to reach out to him whenever needed. He said he was and is always there with me.

"Ask and you shall receive"

Once, at night, I had a vision. The chapter and verse from the bible shown to me was Matthew 7:7. The holy words of Lord Jesus shown to me were, "Ask and you shall receive..." As each word was being written, bright white light could be seen in the background. The light kept increasing, and gently, Lord Jesus appeared in white robes. I was guided that I would be able to experience the real significance of his holy words. Things will happen if I wish. Lord Jesus has always been with me, and I can recollect innumerable incidents.

Lord Jesus's presence can be felt in the church. I go at odd times when the church is empty. I sit there for hours. I don't pray or ask or anything. I find peace there.

Moments with Lord Krishna

Baby Lord Krishna

While meditating on Krishna Janmashtami in 2020, I saw Lord Krishna as a small, cute baby happily eating curd with his small baby hands from an earthen pot.

Lord Krishna Coming Home

Years back, while meditating, Lord Krishna appeared to me. He kept appearing and repeatedly told me that he wanted to come home. I didn't say anything to him initially.

I told him, "I live on rent, and I know once you bring home God's statue, it should not be moved. I will have to move it while shifting."

He smiled and said, "I will come wherever you go. You can talk to me, and I will answer you."

The same year, during our meditation group's special meditation on the 31ˢᵗ of December, Lord Krishna came and sat next to me.

He was smiling and said, "I am very pleased to see your devotion to your Guru." He continued, "I want you to bring a Krishna statue" and showed me the place where I should keep it (next to the holy padukas on the right side)

I told him, "I am not in Bhakti Marg, and I know you are a God. I will ask my Guruji."

He said, "You may ask, but you will have to get it."

He then picked up some flowers, which I had used for decorating. I was looking at him taking the flowers.

He said, "I am taking these flowers, and in return, I bless you with wisdom and wealth."

He then left. All through my meditation, I could feel the energy being received through each breath. It was very peaceful and calm. I was able to breathe very easily through all my chakras.

I asked Guruji, whether I should buy one Lord Krishna statue. Guruji said, "No need now, wait, Om Shanti."

During one of my morning meditations, Lord Krishna appeared and he came and sat beside me, he asked me, "What have you decided?"

I asked him," About what?"

He said, "About keeping my statue." I told him, "I have asked my Guruji. He has told me to wait."

I told him, "I worship only holy padukas, no other Gods. If Guruji allows, I will buy one."

He smiled and said, "I will come with you wherever you go, you can talk to me and I will answer you through the statue."

He said, "You recently had a kundalini awakening. That is why you are having a churning sensation in your throat pit. It is not regular vibrations." He said, "You sing songs for your Guru. Please sing for me."

The words were shown to me, and the song played. I could see and hear:

"Shree Krishna Govind Hare Murari,
Hey Nath Narayan Vasudeva." (thrice), then
"Achyutam Keshavam Krishna Damodaram,
Ram Narayanam Janaki Vallabham" (thrice). Again,
"Shree Krishna Govind Hare Murari,
Hey, Nath Narayan Vasudeva" (thrice).

He lovingly touched my cheek and left.

During our next group meditation, Lord Krishna appeared again. He was very happy and said, "Now you have been chosen to help Nature in any calamity and heal." He said something more that I am not supposed to share. He smiled, kept his hand on my head, and left.

Lord Krishna kept coming. One day, he told me, "Will you accept my statue (that's me) if someone gives it to you as a gift?" I had no answer.

The same day, a member of our meditation group called me up and asked if I could meet her. She said she wanted to gift me Lord Krishna's statue and said she was checking on some idols. She seemed as if she wanted to give it urgently. I told her, "No, wait, let me seek Guruji's permission." Guruji immediately permitted me to accept the statue.

Within a few days, Lord Krishna's idol came home. He talks to me every day, connects with me anytime, anywhere, and guides me on songs too. The statue was divine. He had said many things, and he still conveys many things. Each word said by Lord Krishna is coming true.

I went to the market to buy flowers for the holy padukas and an artificial garland for Lord Krishna, as I knew I wouldn't be doing the rituals. The shopkeeper gave me five peacock feathers along with the garland. When I told him, "I don't need it," he said, "Please take it. You need not pay any money for it."

He didn't accept money, though I requested him. He too refused to take the money and said, "I am not giving it to you. Lord Krishna wants it." I told him "Uncle, I am accepting it, but next time, you please take the money from me." He just smiled.

Same day, after messaging Guruji, during my evening meditation, Lord Krishna appeared. He reduced his size, smiled at me, and merged into the idol; the idol looks divine. I offered flowers, kept jaggery and poha, and put the garland and peacock feather. Lord Krishna is happy.

After my task to help mankind was successful, white light poured at the Sahasrara. I then saw Lord Krishna coming walking down. On either side where he was walking and coming, joined hands could be seen. They were of some rishis or sages. Lord Krishna came and smiled. He was very happy that I had completed the task. He blessed me and gave me a pearl. He went back the same way he came.

Lord Krishna came home when I lived on rent in my previous flat and is with me always. The journey of him coming home was really mystical. He was constantly there with me earlier too. He, all divine, all Gurus chose my new house. It is blessed by all. He guides me on how to handle situations with ease and shows and cautions me from the harm that could be caused by anyone. He is very loving and naughty at times. Sometimes, he plays pranks. He tells me when to clean the idol. Every day, I wipe it with a cloth as guided by him.

Lord Krishna clears all the obstacles and shows his presence or talks to me. Many members of our meditation group had asked me why my morning pranams had changed. My later morning pranams were guided by Lord Krishna. There is so much more, but I am not supposed to reveal anything further.

With Lord Krishna's grace and blessings, I wish to share my happiness: I got a flat of my own and shifted soon. It was gifted to me by a divine soul. The process of getting the flat was miraculous; everything was shown to me in advance.

Lord Krishna's voice from His statue

On a Friday late evening, I was cleaning the place near the holy padukas and Lord Krishna's statue. I heard Lord Krishna's voice from the statue. He wanted to talk to me. I didn't know what to do. First time ever, I heard his voice from the statue. Earlier, I would see or hear him in meditation and was okay with it, now it was reality. I was a bit scared, got up and went to the bedroom.

Dance of Lord Krishna with Gopikas at home

Once, I could sense some movements of footsteps and some noises in the hall. I checked the time; it was past midnight. I was in my bedroom, so I bent down to see from where the noise was heard. It seemed to be a full moon night. The soft white light shone in the entire hall, and I could see Lord Krishna, Maa Radha, and some beautiful girls dressed up in vibrant colours. They were lost in the dance. I kept looking at them for sometime, but I could not move.

At that moment Lord Krishna connected with me saying, "A time will come when you will play with us." Slowly, after a few minutes, while they were playing, they disappeared. After that moment I could move. I went to the hall to check if everything was okay. I felt the place, where they all danced, sacred. I went on for my bath and continued for my day.

The whisper, "wipe my nose"

On Saturday, after dinner, I went and sat near holy padukas, wiped them, removed the flowers which were drying up, and cleaned the place. When I came near Lord Krishna's statue, the strands of the feather started shaking. The fan was off, and the windows were closed.

I started wiping the statue. Lord Krishna softly whispered, "Wipe my nose." I wiped his nose, cleaned the statue, closed my eyes, and sat.

He said, "I want two things: first wipe my idol daily; second, sit and talk to me."

The shaking of peacock feather

One day, after evening meditation, as soon as I went near the statue, the peacock feather strands again started shaking. The statue was smiling and happy. The feathers shake only till I sit; after that, the whole day, this doesn't happen, even if the fan is on or the window is open.

Baby Lord Krishna in a wooden cart

While meditating, I saw many wooden carts joined to each other. They were moving as a mini train. The carts were carrying large mud pots full of milk and curd. The carts keep passing. Among one of the carts, I saw Lord Krishna as a baby sitting in one of the pots, smiling at me. He had little curd near his mouth and on his fingers too. He looked very cute.

Lord Krishna asking for curd

While meditating, I felt Lord Krishna's presence and then heard his voice. He happily asked me to offer him Makhan, then said,

"No. It will be adulterated; you offer me curd." He even showed me the bowl in which he wanted it to be served to him.

I asked him, "I don't eat curd, if I offer it to you, who will eat it after offering?"

He told me "Don't worry. You just offer it to me. I will finish it up." I could see him smiling. I said, "I will offer it to you."

He wanted it to be served on a Thursday. This was the first time he had asked for something as offering. I didn't write to Guruji seeking permission to buy as it was Thursday. Guruji had asked all members to maintain silence on Thursday. I then bought curd and served it in the bowl, along with a spoon which was shown to me.

I kept it near the idol, closed my eyes, and said, "Lord Krishna please accept my humble offering." As soon as said, I heard the noise of the spoon. I didn't open my eyes. After a few minutes, I opened my eyes and saw the position of the spoon was not the same, and the quantity of curd was less. I then got up and went to the bedroom. I came back after a while; the quantity of curd had again reduced. So, I added a little more, it happened two to three times. Almost half of the pack of curd was consumed by Lord Krishna. He seemed happy and was smiling through the idol. I discarded the remaining curd.

Lord Krishna's dance on hoods of Kaliya

One morning, while meditating, I saw Lord Krishna as a young boy dancing and jumping on the hoods of a huge, multi-hooded, deadly snake in a river. The name shown was Yamuna River. He kept breaking the snake's hoods one by one. The name of the snake shown to me was Kaliya. The snake tried to coil around Lord Krishna and fight back. Lord Krishna went underwater, but nothing happened to him.

Kaliya then said, "You have created me and other good things. What is my fault?"

Lord Krishna said, "I will not kill you. You leave this place, as you have troubled many." Kaliya agreed and left the river.

Let the fan be on

One afternoon, as usual, I went to switch off the fan in the hall.

I heard Lord Krishna's voice in my ears softly telling me, "It's hot. Let the fan be on. This is not an idol at home. I am present here."

The peacock feather was shaking. Since then, I have kept the fan on day and night. Only while meditating, I keep it very slow.

The Song – Bada Natkhat hai re

There are times when my heart is overflowing with love and gratitude. When I sit for meditation, some songs are shown to me. They are the exact words of what I feel like expressing and then I am guided to sing.

After coming back from a retreat, while meditating, I felt Guruji's mother's presence. She wanted me to convey her message to Guruji. She said she felt sad seeing him crying at our retreat remembering her. She said she loves him a lot and if memories hurt him, not to speak as she can't see him crying. She lovingly touched my left cheek, kissed both my cheeks, blessed me, and said, "There's a lot you have to do." She smiled and left.

After she left, I could hear a song that kept playing repeatedly and still continued to play. It went like this (in Hindi):

"Bada Natkhat hai re Krishna Kanhaiya,

ka Karen Yashoda Maiya"

I could feel a mother's pure love to her son while hearing the song. The song was shown to me. While recording the song "Bada Natkhat hai ...," I had to record it a few times. Some mistakes kept happening. I then went and sat near Lord Krishna's statue. The feather started shaking. I said, "Lord Krishna, I know you are playing a prank with me. Please help me record it. I want to dedicate it to my Guruji and his dear mother." I could feel Lord Krishna's presence. I then sang the song, and the recording was perfect.

Another day, while meditating in the morning, I felt Guruji's mother's presence. She gently kept her hand on my head and moved her hand from the front of my head to the back very delicately a few times. She then lovingly said, "You have sung the song. Now post it." Saying this, she left.

The song - Hare Krishna Hare Krishna

I shared my experience of how I couldn't record the song Bada Natkhat hai, till I went and sat near Lord Krishna's idol and asked for help, knowing he was playing a prank as I would get stuck on the word "Krishnan Kanhaiya." That time, after I recorded "Bada Natkhat hai," he had immediately shown me a song:

"Hare Krishna Hare Krishna,

Krishna Krishna Hare Hare.

Hare Rama Hare Rama,

Rama Rama Hare Hare." I had not posted the song, so I was reminded again in meditation to sing and post it. After the songs are shown to me, I check on YouTube for the tune and record it.

The beginning of offering flowers

During one of our group meditations, I was guided by Lord Krishna to remove the artificial garland which was around the idol. I had put the garland as I wasn't sure if I would offer him flowers every day.

Whenever I would do paduka pooja, he would very lovingly ask me to offer him flowers, only flowers having fragrance or flowers yellow in colour. He showed me the flowers that he likes. He is very happy as I started offering flowers to him after the paduka pooja. Lord Krishna talks to me daily and guides me. He is very happy.

The Song - Jya jya thikani man jaye maaze

A beautiful divine experience with Lord Krishna. A day before Janmashtami, Lord Krishna spoke to me through his idol and asked me to serve him curd the next day. He even showed me the bowl and spoon.

While I was serving curd in a bowl to be offered to him, a song began to play in my ears. Even after offering the curd, the song kept going on for a while. Late evening, I came to know it was a song dedicated to Lord Krishna. He wanted me to share it in our meditation group. It is a song in Marathi. I wasn't sure if I would be able to sing the complete song.

Earlier, I shared a few lines in Marathi that were shown to me by Swami Samarth. It goes like this:

"Jya jya thikani man jaye majhe,

tya tya thikani nij Roop tujhe,

me thevito mastak jya thikani,

tethe tujhe sadhuru paye doni"

But this time, it was a complete song. I tried singing it and shared it in our meditation group. I have never heard this song before.

After a few hours, when I went to lift the bowl, the curd quantity had reduced. Thinking he must have finished eating,

I tried to remove the spoon before lifting the bowl. The spoon was tightly stuck to the bowl, and he was smiling through the idol.

He softly spoke to me saying, "Let it be. I will have it". Soon, the curd turned to butter, and he consumed almost everything.

This has happened many times. The curd offered to him turns to butter in no time, and he consumes it. Sometimes, he just has the curd.

For Polish of Idol, "I am not going anywhere"

Lord Krishna's statue is made up of different metals. After a few days of cleaning it with natural ingredients, it turns dark, and its shine fades out. I felt that if I got the statue polished, the shine would remain for a longer period. I spoke to someone who was ready to polish the idol. He asked me to bring the statue over, as the polishing cannot be done at home.

I sought Lord Krishna's guidance, he then told me, "You can enquire if they can polish the idol at home. I am not going anywhere."

Entry to my new house

In meditation, a few days before the 11th, I was guided to step into the new house on the 11th at 11 a.m. and shift the same day. On the 10th, they declared Maharashtra Bandh would be observed the next day, on the 11th.

I was sure that the bandh wouldn't affect my shifting, still, I called up the tempo guy and asked him if he was willing to the come next day, as the bandh had been declared, and they were announcing on speakers to keep everything shut.

He said, "I will come. Even if it's a bandh, I will come tomorrow with my relatives. Don't worry, the shifting will be done tomorrow."

Next day, I left for the new place with holy padukas, Lord Krishna's idol, and some more things. No cops stopped me. To my surprise, I got flowers.

There was an uncle selling flowers outside a Shiva temple, very close to my previous flat. I had never seen him before. He gave me lots of flowers, some bel and Tulsi leaves. I asked him for a particular flower that Lord Krishna likes and asks me to offer. He said they are over. I thanked him, as getting flowers would be difficult with everything was closed.

He gave me the flowers in a bag and said, "I have put the flowers in the bag, including the ones which you asked for"

I told him, "Uncle, you didn't have them, and I didn't see you putting them in." He said, "They are there." I checked the bag. They were really there.

I thanked him once again, paid, and left. I was in a hurry as I didn't want to be late. Lord Krishna was very happy, connected with me, and said, "Be peaceful. I can stop the time for you."

I bought milk on the way to boil it over. When I reached the building, there were a few minutes left for 11 a.m. Lord Krishna, smilingly, again connected, saying, "What better muhurat than 11 hours, 11 minutes, and 11 seconds on the 11th?"

Quickly, I decorated the padukas and offered some fruits, flowers, and curd to Lord Krishna. Also, I offered flowers to Gurus lamp.

One of my friends had told me to boil milk in a new vessel and allow a little milk to overflow. She said it is a ritual that people follow when they start to stay in a new house. I bought a new vessel and milk. On entering my house, I offered flowers to all divine and curd to Lord Krishna as asked by him. I then switched on the gas knob to ignite the gas stove; the gas stove didn't work.

The gas stove was a surprise gift that was delivered to the watchman of my previous flat. The watchman told me a delivery guy hurriedly handed it over to him. He said he accepted it as the name and address was perfect. He brought it home, and I had checked it before shifting. It was working well then.

Now, while the gas wasn't working, I could see Lord Krishna smiling. I wondered, "Why is he smiling?" I poured the milk into the vessel and carried on with my work. After a while, upon checking, I noticed the milk had turned into thick curd; it resembled a thick chunk of paneer. Just then, Lord Krishna showed me a bowl and a spoon. He guided me to open the kitchen drawer and take a specific bowl and spoon that were new, to serve him curd. At that moment, I understood why the gas knob didn't turn on. This was the first gift that I had received from him before shifting to the new house.

The tempo guy came with his uncle and said, "Ma'am, my uncle has bought a new tempo. We are from Ayodhya. This is my first order." He alone, non-stop, kept carrying the stuff, except for the cupboard, and wasn't tired at all. I have lived my life on rent and have shifted many times. I never saw anyone single-handedly doing so much work with a smile on his face. Though it was raining, he safely shifted my things without damaging or letting anything get wet.

Before shifting, I was guided by Lord Krishna that gifts would keep coming and that I should keep accepting them without thinking. I shared with Guruji about my shifting, and also what Lord Krishna had said to me, and asked him for his guidance. Guruji's reply made me overjoyed; as Guruji's guidance and Lord Krishna's guidance were alike. Mother Nature was showering love and blessings upon me. Her blessings started pouring in, in different forms in abundance. I didn't know who the angels were. The universe was showering love and blessings upon me. This began to happen after I received Lord Krishna's guidance.

Earlier too things which I needed would be dropped at my doorstep. I would be amazed, because, except me, no one else knew what I needed.

The Curd Maestro

Before shifting, I went to purchase a fridge (it was gifted) as the one I was using was having some problems. Somehow, I didn't know why, I straight away went to a particular fridge, had a look at it, and liked its interior. It had good space, better than what I had. It had a compartment to form curd. I was told it was a newly launched "Curd Maestro" I had a thought: "Everything is fine, but the compartment for making curd is taking up some space."

The sales representative guided me to see another model, saying, "Since you don't require cold water or curd, buy this one as it has more space." While giving a demo, he shared his troubles with me. He told me that he wasn't able to sell any products and that he was new to Mumbai. His job was in danger, and if I purchased it, his job would be safe. I felt sad for him and said, "Don't worry, I'll buy it." All the while, my mind was still stuck on "Curd Maestro." I wondered, "Why? Was it an indication by Lord Krishna to buy one?"

I checked both the fridges a couple of times and thought of helping the representative. He was very happy and thanked me. The fridge came home, and while it was getting installed, I was still shown the "Curd Maestro". Now I was sure Lord Krishna wanted it to come home. I asked Lord Krishna to give me an indication if he wanted it.

Within a second, the technician found a fault and said, "Ma'am, the product is damaged," and showed me the damaged part. He clicked the photos; gave me a customer service report card mentioning the damage, and told me, "You can ask for an exchange." Happily, I went to the showroom and showed the same representative the pictures. I asked him if I could book the "Curd Maestro" model.

He said, "It's out of stock. You may see another model." I told him, "I want to go only with the 'Curd Maestro', nothing else." He said, "We can give you a credit voucher, you can use it within six months to buy anything." I told him, "Please try to understand, I need a fridge. The voucher will be of no use to me."

I requested them to refund. The salesman said, "We can replace the product, we don't offer a refund, but I will make sure your money will be refunded." He spoke to his higher-ups, and came to the counter and requested the cashier to issue a refund, mentioning the reason: "The product bought was damaged, and now the item wanted is out of stock." He continued, "Refund Ma'am the money."

The cashier said, "It's against our policy." The representative replied, "The senior has signed the voucher." The money was refunded. The representative told me "Ma'am please count the money." I told him, "I trust you." I thanked him and he thanked me too.

At that time, Curd Maestro was out of stock in all branches across India. All online apps showed it was unavailable.

After I received the refund, I checked online, and luckily, one fridge suddenly showed as available. I immediately booked it, and it came home the next day. When it came home, he was very happy.

Nahi to main Chori karke Kha loonga

Some years ago, on a Wednesday evening, with a smile, Lord Krishna said, "I want you to serve me curd tomorrow". The next day, early morning, while I was cleaning the place where holy padukas, Lord Krishna's idol, and Gurus lamp are kept, he connected, saying, "Mujhe nahana hai aur dahi khana hai." (I need to take a bath and eat curd)

Towards the end of my meditation, he reminded me in a naughty mood, saying,"Nahane ke baad Mujhe dahi dena, bhoolna mat, nahi to main chori kar ke kha loonga." (Give me curd after my bath, don't forget; otherwise, I'll steal it and eat it) Saying this, he happily left.

I offered him the curd set in the Curd Maestro. He ate it happily. Unbelievable but true, the quantity of curd kept reducing, and I kept adding more. I later on gave the remaining to someone.

I am overwhelmed by his love, sweet pranks, the warmth, support, miracles, and the grace that he showers on me. He is very compassionate.

The drawer that got stuck

I do not have much knowledge of all the Gods and Goddesses. I am still learning. They reveal their names when they appear. Sometimes, they reveal the purpose of their visit.

One afternoon, I went to the kitchen to serve my lunch along with ginger-garlic paste. I cleaned the ginger and garlic and kept it aside. I tried opening the kitchen drawer to get the mortar and pestle out to make the ginger-garlic paste. The drawer was stuck and wasn't opening more than two inches. I slipped my hand in through the gap to check as to why it wasn't opening. I realised the edges of a steel bowl were stuck on the upper part of the drawer. For a few minutes, I tried to drop the bowl into the drawer with my fingers, a spoon, and a rolling pin, but nothing worked. I then thought, "It's fine, I will chew the ginger-garlic, wouldn't be able to chop as the knives were also in the drawer."

Just then, I could hear a few words being repeated. The words were: "Om Namo Bhagavate Vasudevaya." I could see Lord Krishna smiling at me. Instantly, I remembered his divine guidance of calling out to him. On checking this time, the drawer opened effortlessly, and the bowl fell into the drawer. My problem was solved.

Bhagavad Gita coming home

Almost three years ago, our family friend had a visitor at his shop. He was a small boy of about 8 to 9 years of age. He was fair and had a cute, smiling face, and brown eyes. He had worn spectacles, a kurta, pants, and chappals. He carried a cloth bag on his shoulder.

The child asked our family friend if he would like to read the Bhagavad Gita. He continued to say, "I have it in all languages. Which one would you prefer?" Our family friend replied, "I don't read holy books."

Just then, the thought of asking me came to his mind. He called me up and told me about the little boy selling Bhagavad Gita. He also told me that the Bhagavad Gita is all about Lord Krishna and asked me if he could buy one and in which language. While asking me, he told the child to give him an English version and asked him how much he had to pay. The little boy happily smiled and asked for a small amount.

As soon as our family friend turned to remove money from the drawer, the little boy kept the book on the counter and disappeared within seconds. Our family friend came out of his shop and looked for him. The boy was nowhere to be seen. He enquired about the small boy with the neighbouring shops. They said no child had come to their shop.

He handed over the book to me and said, "I felt he was Lord Krishna in disguise. He wanted to give you the Bhagavad Gita to know him better. He was smiling all the time. How could he have books in all languages? Why did the thought of asking you come to my mind? Why did he come only to my shop to give the book and disappear without taking any money? I feel the book had to reach you, and I was the medium."

I told him, "Lord Krishna will guide and answer all the questions. Thank you." I took the book and kept it near Lord Krishna's idol. He was smiling through the idol. I got my answer. Same evening, in meditation, Lord Krishna confirmed, that it was him indeed.

He continued and guided me on reading the Bhagavad Gita.

New World

Once, while meditating, Lord Krishna asked me if I was ready to go to the new world which is being created. He told me I would be the first person to be going there if I said yes. I told him, "I wish to wait here for some time, but if you feel that's good for me, I will follow whatever you say." He just smiled.

Vishwaroopa

Once, during meditation, while talking to me, Lord Krishna began to increase in size. He became huge, and I looked very tiny in front of him. Slowly, I could see him with innumerable hands holding different articles and with heads of all the Gods. I could see his Sudarshan chakra and mace. He was looking at me. I didn't get scared at all, as I had seen him enlarge in size and knew it was Lord Krishna doing it.

Another day, while meditating, Lord Krishna told me, "Today I wish to show you myself in multiple forms, called Vishwaroopa. Don't get scared."

I told him, "I won't. I had seen you earlier too and didn't get frightened."

He began to grow in size. This time I saw multiple universes, galaxies, and gods emerging from him. There were many hands and heads joined to him, as I had seen earlier. I looked in amazement as to how vast one can be. He looked at me and smiled.

Precious Stone from Lord Krishna's Ajna

One day, when I sought blessings from Lord Krishna, He began to smile. From his Ajna, a white precious stone emitting bright light came out. He kept looking at me and lovingly said, "Join your palms and accept it." I joined my palms exactly the same way we accepted Prasad. The stone slowly came and fell into my hands. He asked me to sit near him after sometime.

Fog-like formation behind Lord Krishna Idol

On an evening, while meditating, my eyes on the own opened, and I could see fog or smoke-like formation behind Lord Krishna's idol. It appeared as if he was coming in person. I swiftly closed my eyes and continued meditating. After meditation when I opened my eyes, the entire hall had a slight fog. I went to the kitchen to check if there was any problem. Everything seemed fine. The fog was only in the hall.

Lord Krishna Happily Dancing to my song

Once, when I chanted "Gurur Brahma Gurur Vishnu…," and, on my own, I began to sing, "Hare Krishna…," Instantly, I saw Lord Krishna smiling and dancing happily playing with a peacock. He seemed to be enjoying me singing the song for him. The peacock feathers placed near his idol began to shake and looked very beautiful.

Feather turned circles

I saw a beautiful peacock feather at the Anahata chakra during an evening meditation. After a moment, I could see some images on the feather. The image was not clear. Slowly, the feather began to turn in circles. Then, the feather disappeared, and I could see Lord Krishna's smiling face for a few seconds.

Govardhan Hill

Once, during my evening meditation, I could see a hill with a lot of greenery and beautiful flowers in pink, white, and crimson red. Many cows could be seen. Slowly the surroundings were revealed to me. I could hear the sweet sound of a flute being played. Lord Krishna could be seen standing on a mound of earth smilingly playing his flute. As he was playing cows began to gather around the mound. All the cows were white. After a while, they spread in different directions, grazing, sitting, or walking around. To Lord Krishna's left, a very pretty girl could be seen playing on a swing, tied between two trees. I was shown she is Radha. There were many girls near her dressed in vibrant colours playing. Near Lord Krishna too, there were many girls. They all seemed on cloud nine. Simultaneously Lord Krishna's voice could be heard He told me; he was on the Govardhan hill. The name Govardhan Hill was highlighted in front of my eyes. He continued, that this is the place where he used to spend his time with his friends. He said he wanted me to see the place where he spent his days, so happily he showed it to me. The place appeared mystical. Slowly, things blurred and I continued meditating peacefully.

Lord Krishna's guidance on Ashwathama

Once, as I began to meditate, I saw a tall well-built man wandering in the jungle of the Himalayas (the word "Himalayas" was shown to me).

He had worn an orange dhoti an orange cloth across his shoulder. He had Rudraksha beads around his neck, arms, and wrist. His eyes were sharp and powerful. He had a mark on his forehead at the Ajna chakra. It appeared as a wound.

He seemed restless and in pain and had some sores on his body. My heart chakra went out and reached in front of the person.

He looked at me and said, "I am wandering for peace." He was disturbed. He told me, "I wander, then meditate, then wander. All my life I am wandering. Only a few can see me. I am Ashwathama."

He continued, "You are good, unlike me. You follow the right path. I cannot even bless you. Grant me peace if you can." Saying this, he walked away. My soul came back, and I continued to meditate. I was shown he was the son of a sage Dronacharya, who had done penance to please Lord Shiva to have a son with the qualities Lord Shiva has. Lord Shiva granted him the boon, and thus Ashwathama was born. He is immortal.

Immediately, Lord Krishna guided me, "He is undergoing suffering for his karmas." I was shown what he did and why he is suffering. I was shown that no one is spared for their wrongdoing.

I have never heard or read about Ashwathama. I recollected everything after meditation and noted the experience.

And the journey with Lord Krishna carries on…

Divine Encounters with Lord Ram, Maa Sita, and Hanuman

Darshan of Shree Rama and Mata Sita in Lord Hanuman's chest

As I began meditation, I saw a flying vehicle outside the window. I was shown that it's called vahana of the Gods. I then saw someone swiftly flying and coming in. He came in holding a large mace(gada), which seemed very heavy. He was holding it in his right hand across his shoulders.

He was part human and part monkey. He had a crown or mukut on his head, the face of a monkey. His face was red. He had a long tail and large kadas on both his wrists and ankles. He had worn a loincloth around his waist.

He bent down, and kept his gada next to him, went down on his knees, joined his hands, bowed, and did pranams to Lord Krishna. I could see Lord Krishna smiling and blessing him. I was shown that he was Hanuman. He looked at me meditating and sat for a while next to me.

He then stood up and opened his chest with both his hands. I could see two people inside. He told me they are Shree Rama and Mata Sita. They both were smiling. They blessed me.

He then closed his chest and said, "I have some powers; I can give them to you." He then tapped me twice very gently on my Sahasrara Chakra, picked his mace or gada, and flew out of the window. As he left, the flying vehicle which I had seen also disappeared.

Lord Rama Blessed me and gave me a flower

Lord Rama appeared in my meditation and gave his divine darshan and blessings. Although I had received his blessings in meditation before, this time he seemed very happy. He gave me a flower and blessed me.

Hanuman blessed me and gave orange Laddu

During a Thursday meditation, Lord Hanuman came home. He came from the window and stood near the window. He saw me meditating and said, "I have brought something for you." Happily, with a smiling face, he gave me an orange laddu, blessed me, and said, "I am in a hurry; I have to go urgently. I have to go." He left immediately.

Lord Hanuman Comes to Meet Me

One morning, I took an auto to an ATM, but my usual route was under repair. So, I asked the driver to take a different one. At a signal, I saw a massive cardboard cutout of Lord Hanuman, as tall as a three-storeyed building, something I'd never seen in Mumbai. When I reached the ATM, it was closed. Instead of turning back, I decided to walk a bit further. A little ahead, I noticed a cute little boy, around 4 or 5 years old, sitting alone on a bus stop bench.

He was dressed in Lord Hanuman's costume, holding a mace, and was smiling. I looked around, but there was no elder with him. He sat alone. I wondered why such a small child was moving around alone.

At that moment, I noticed a shop with a glass door displaying various dates, including the ones Guruji had recommended years ago. Never before had I found these dates available in any nearby shops, and my attempts to order them online were unsuccessful. Remembering Guruji's precious guidance, I entered the shop to buy the dates.

When I stepped out of the shop, the child was still sitting alone. I was concerned and turned to see if any relatives or family members were with the boy. He was happily playing with his mace, radiating a powerful positive energy. I felt blissful seeing him and thought of blessing him, but I couldn't move and was suddenly drawn to taking an auto home. As I got in the auto and turned back, the boy had vanished. I asked the driver to stop, got down, and looked around, but he was nowhere to be seen. With goosebumps, I continued home.

On the way, I stopped to buy some flowers. The flower lady filled my bag with many types of yellow flowers and Tulsi (holy basil) leaves. I told the flower seller the bag was full, but she handed it to me and asked for only Rs.20. She looked into my eyes and said, "Shri Krishna likes yellow."

Instantly, I remembered Guruji blessing me, saying, "You have Lord Krishna with you. You have everything. You will keep getting in abundance." I thanked her and continued home.

In the evening, before meditation, for the first time, I asked for strength without praying to any specific deity. During meditation, I saw dense forests and Lord Hanuman meditating. He opened his eyes, smiled at me, and revealed his current location.

He said, "I came to give you darshan, but you ignored me." In a flash, I remembered the huge cutout of Lord Hanuman and realised what he meant.

He continued, "Since you didn't notice me, I came again. Yes, it was me," referring to the child. "I am also called Anjani Putra. The colour orange is connected with a Guru." I recalled the boy in orange clothes. He explained that if he had approached me, people would have noticed, so he sat where no one paid attention.

"My purpose to meet you would be disturbed," he said.

Reading my mind of blessing him, he smiled and asked, "How could you bless me? Is that possible?" He diverted my mind to going home to avoid a crowd.

He then showed me a rare leaf and instructed me to look for it. "If you see it anywhere, consume one leaf. You may find it with a flower seller who won't know or understand it, but you may recognize it. I will not tell you the name, as you might share it by mistake. If you happen to get the plant, buy it; else, I will come and give it to you." Saying this, he blessed me and disappeared.

Lord Rama and Lord Krishna are seen together

Once, while meditating, I saw a blue arm with an amulet and the back of a God. I could also see a quiver in which arrows are kept. Soon, I realised he was Lord Rama. He then showed his face and presence. He was at the left of Lord Krishna's idol, smiling at me. Lord Krishna too was smiling through the idol.

My Connection with Lord Shiva and Maa Parvati

Protected By Lord Shiva

As a child, I had a repeated dream of being carefully protected and taken care by serpents. My father took me to an ancient Shiva temple to seek answers about what these dreams interpreted.

The temple priest told my father, "Things will unfold at the right time. She is a blessed child. One thing is sure, she is protected by Shiva"

Darshan of the union of Lord Shiva and Parvati

Once, during meditation, I saw the union of Lord Shiva and Goddess Parvati and kumkum, curd, water, milk, honey, and flowers being offered to the Shiva Linga. I received a flower as a blessing. From nowhere, it fell into my hands.

At Kailash

During the initial months when Corona had started, I saw myself in Kailash. Maa Parvati said to Lord Shiva, "Look who has come," and she put a tiger's skin and made me sit on it. I could see my real self. I asked Lord Shiva, "How long have I to be, and suffer, on earth? Please help the people." Lord Shiva didn't answer. I said "I am going, but will come back for an answer" and came back.

Ardhanarishwar

In an evening meditation, I saw a single body divided exactly into two halves. To the right was Lord Shiva one side and to the left Maa Parvati could be seen. Their aura was very powerful, and they took me in their aura. I had seen Ardhanarishwar earlier too, during my initial days of meditation, and had received their blessings. At that time, I didn't know they are addressed as Ardhanarishwar.

Ardhanarishwar Portrait Coming Home

One day, just after shifting to the current flat in which I am staying, I had a divine meditation experience. I experienced Lord Shiva's presence.

He told me, "You will soon receive a gift. Accept it."

After some days, one of my friend's relative, an excellent artist painted a portrait. She had never done such a painting before. Seeing the portrait, my friend expressed her wish to gift it to me.

She said, "Even if you say no, I will get it to your place. It is made for you."

Remembering Lord Shiva's guidance, I said yes to her. It was a large portrait packed very neatly. On opening it, I was awestruck. It was a portrait of Ardhanarishwar.

Immediately, I received an insight, it was the same gift that was supposed to reach me. The portrait is beautiful and divine.

Before gifting it to me, the artist had clicked a photo and shared it with some people. They liked it and at once requested her to make the same, in different sizes. She told me that after multiple attempts, she just couldn't paint it the same way again.

I offered my deepest gratitude to both and to Guruji, as the alarm rang, signalling the end of my meditation.

Moments with Lord Shiva

Lord Shiva said to me, "I am there behind you."

During one of my meditations, I could see myself at Kedarnath and coming back. Soon, I saw Lord Shiva coming home, he said, "You have your Guru in front of you, and I am there behind you."

Flower as blessing from Lord Shiva

I saw Abhishek of the Shiva Lingam. I was sitting alone and watching while the pooja was going on. A flower fell into my lap from nowhere. I felt blessed to receive his blessings.

Liquid from his Kamandal as blessing from Lord Shiva

A few months back, I saw myself at Kailash. Lord Shiva was happy to see me. He took me on his lap and gave me some liquid to drink from a rare pot with a handle (the name shown as Kamandal) which was near him. I have had this experience a few times on different days.

Lord Shiva came to take me to his Holy Abode

Lord Shiva had given me his divine Darshan and had asked me to come to his Holy Abode for three days continuously. I had forgotten about it, so he came to take me.

Once, during morning meditation, I saw myself at the border. I saw soldiers, their tents, snow-capped mountains, and conical trees. I then saw myself as a small child, and Lord Shiva coming, holding my hand, and taking me away.

He walked with me up to a point, and then there appeared a plate of milk. He told me to dip my feet for cleansing and took me along. It later appeared as a lake close to snow-capped mountains. He took me there and made me sit on the peak of the mountain. He was teaching me how to meditate. I moved a bit, and he put his hand behind me so that I may not fall. I was in a naughty mood so I tried to do it again by bending my body backward. He smiled, removed his hand, and said, "Now you will not fall." I really didn't. I then sat back straight and meditated fervently as he taught me. My soul happily came back.

Rudraksha Mala Blessing from Lord Shiva

I saw Lord Shiva in meditation one evening. I could see blue everywhere, and then suddenly, I saw him. He came, tied my hair up, put Rudraksha mala in my hair and around my neck, and blessed me.

Lord Shiva told me to ask what I want

Once, in morning meditation, I saw Lord Shiva. While meditating, I received his Darshan (vision) and blessings. His presence could be felt for some time. He told me to ask for what I wanted. I didn't ask for anything and was in a trance state the entire day.

Lord Shiva's guidance to wear Rudraksha Mala

One Sunday, out of nowhere, I found a Rudraksha in my bedroom. I didn't buy it, nor did anyone give it to me. Before I found it, for the past few days, I was continuously guided by Lord Shiva in meditation to wear a Rudraksha mala. Also, almost one and a half year back, while meditating, I had seen a Rudraksha coming out of Lord Shiva's hand. It rolled and came to me.

Lord Shiva sending me energy in the form of light as protection

During a morning meditation, I saw Lord Shiva. He was meditating. He slowly opened his eyes and started sending me energy, it appeared as light. I felt the light very powerful. I was covered from head to feet in it.

As the energy kept flowing from the Sahasrara to my whole body, I got goosebumps. My body was shaking. I could feel the light as a protection. A shield was formed around me, and I was enclosed in it. I was in a happy state. Lord Shiva then closed his eyes and continued meditating.

Lord Shiva Wrapped me in tiger skin

During an evening meditation, I received Lord Shiva's darshan. I saw Lord Shiva coming home. He was holding his trident and looked magnificent. He looked at me. He had a tiger skin around his waist, which he slightly pulled. It kept unwrapping, and he kept wrapping me in it. I was completely covered with it.

He then reduced his size and sat next to me for a few seconds. While leaving, he turned back. He looked too powerful. I could feel high energy in my body. My eyes kept closing. I continued to sit on my meditation mat till I felt fine.

The welcome I received at Kailash

While meditating, I saw myself amidst the snow. I stood looking around. I knew I was in Kailash, as I have been there many times in meditation.

I saw strange-looking beings. Among them, one was half man and half bull. He had worn a necklace with a bell and some ornaments. He had three horizontal lines on his forehead. He had a plate in his hand with some pooja articles. I was shown that he is Nandi, the gatekeeper of Kailash and the vahana/vehicle of Lord Shiva. The beings with him are the Ganas. Behind these beings, I saw Mount Kailash. It appeared huge and majestic in the background, and we were at its foothills.

They came to me happily dancing. Nandi held the pooja thali, put a tilak on my forehead, circled the pooja thali thrice around me, and garlanded me with Chafa/Plumeria flowers (like what Lord Shiva had given me in an earlier meditation). He said, "Welcome, we were waiting for you." They kept dancing around me for some time. Just then, I saw Lord Shiva. He appeared very huge and was in meditation. Slowly, the snow on one portion of Mount Kailash started to make way, uncovering a door that was hidden underneath. It appeared as if the door was made of gold in intricate design. After a while, the door opened and the beings rushed in. The door closed, and snow covered it, such that it was out of sight. Lord Shiva was undisturbed throughout this entire experience. He was in deep meditation.

Lord Shiva stretching his hands from Kailash to my home

While meditating, I saw Lord Shiva stretching his hand from Kailash to my home and giving me a tiny black seed. He told me to consume it, and I did. He smiled at me.

Lord Shiva Gave me Amrut

Once while meditating, I saw part of a wall in blue colour, and next to the wall was a pot with a plant having only green leaves. Then, I felt a presence near me, slightly ahead of me, to my right side. Soon, I saw two legs below the knees. The legs were blue in colour. Next, I saw a bit of tiger skin worn above the knees. I was sure then that he was Lord Shiva as I had received his darshan in this form several times earlier.

It appeared as if he was passing by from my right side. Slowly, I saw heavy kadas (anklets), at his ankles. Gradually, I started seeing him all above the knees.

He turned back and looked at me. He was massive! He picked me up with his left hand and cradled me in his arms. He had a pitcher (kamandal) filled with Amrut in the right hand. He very gently held the pitcher to my mouth and made me drink the Amrut.

I saw myself as a tiny tot in perhaps my true soul form. He then lovingly put me back on my meditation mat and went away.

Lord Shiva offering Me a Special Boon

Once, a few minutes before I began to meditate, a sweet, rare, and heavenly fragrance filled the room, it was not from the flowers. During meditation, each and every part of my body started vibrating, and I could see the cells of my body vibrating. Divine light filled my body, and my chakras rotated in sync at high speed. Divine energy filled my Sushumna Nadi, rising from the Mooladhara and reaching the Sahasrara.

Instantly, I felt Lord Shiva's presence; he was standing next to me. My head reached the lower calf of his leg. He gently placed his hand on my Sahasrara Chakra, and an open lotus in rainbow colours appeared on my head from nowhere. He blessed me with a boon, which he said, will soon manifest into reality.

Monk Milerapa

In a meditation, a monk appeared to me. I received his blessings. His name, shown to me, was Milerapa. He didn't speak but conveyed his thoughts, through written words which I could see and read. It went like this, "I have climbed Mount Kailash. I felt to visit you; to tell you, that I had a lot of hardships before reaching to the top. Only the chosen can reach him. People forcibly try to reach Shiva; disasters happen."

Initial Astral Travel Experiences with Lord Shiva

During one of my morning meditations, I saw a flame at the center of my chest (Anahata chakra). The next day, I saw a flame at the Ajna chakra. On the third day, I saw a flame at the Sahasrara chakra. I didn't know what it meant. After two days, while meditating early in the morning, I saw an opening at the Ajna Chakra and was pulled in. I passed through Nature, reached snow-clad mountains, and saw Lord Shiva. He was meditating. He appeared huge. I was scared to go in front of him, as he was meditating, and I didn't want to disturb him. I received an insight to go and sit in front of him. I followed the guidance. Soon, my soul came back. After a while, I saw the flame from the Anahata chakra and Ajna chakra coming out and slowly merging with the flame at the Sahasrara chakra, at the top of my head forming a single flame. The process of all the flames merging was mesmerizing.

Divine Encounters with Lord Buddha

Lord Buddha smiling at me

While meditating I saw myself meditating near a stream in a forest. Slowly, the water levels began to increase. I was getting covered inch by inch and was completely submerged. The water appeared crystal clear. After a while, I saw myself rising up in a meditative pose and floating above the water. Slowly, the water receded and I came down. I could feel someone's presence. After meditating, when I opened my eyes, I saw Lord Buddha smiling at me. He blessed me.

Lord Buddha blessed me

I saw Buddha while meditating. He came and sat beside me. He seemed happy. While leaving, he tore a piece of cloth from the robe which was around his shoulders, and put it around my neck. He placed a few gemstones on my lap and left.

Lord Buddha blessed me with a lotus

During one of my evening meditations, I saw Lord Buddha sitting on a pink lotus and meditating. After sometime, he got up, picked up the lotus, happily gave it to me, and left.

Lord Buddha taught me meditation mudra

A few days back, Lord Buddha came, took my hands during meditation, and placed them on one top of the other in my lap. My thumbs were touching each other. He said to meditate keeping the hands this way. I was having blissful experiences with Lord Shiva, Lord Buddha, and some saints and receiving their blessings.

Lord Buddha's two hands at Sahasrara

Once, during my morning meditation, I saw two hands at the Sahasrara. The hands were pouring pearls at the Sahasrara. All the pearls were of the same size and colour. Then, I saw a precious stone at the Sahasrara. It was emitting very bright light. There was tremendous brightness around me, and I was encircled with divine light. The white light kept pouring at the Sahasrara. The surroundings were blue.

Later, a crown was placed on my head, it was not the normal crown we see, it was different. I could see the two hands were of Lord Buddha. He was smiling.

My Name added to the Book of All Saints

During my morning meditation, I saw Lord Buddha coming through the window. He had a half open book in his hand. It seemed very old and heavy.

He came and sat beside me and said, "What name should I add to the book Shashtria or Sruthi?"

I didn't reply, as I didn't know what it was.

He then said, "Sruthi," and wrote my name.

To the left of the name, he put a photo of mine, it was the same photo clicked during my second-level initiation.

He said "Your name is added to the book of all saints and holy men whom people follow in meditation. The ones who know you can ask you to guide them. You have reached a high level." He blessed me and said, "You can call out to me anytime for guidance."

Guruji acknowledged my above experience and gave me his blessings.

A leaf from Bodhi Tree

One day, my early morning routine was completed very fast. I was on my meditation mat at 3.45 a.m. That specific day, I was guided by Lord Buddha to meditate at exactly 4.44 a.m. So, I sat on my meditation mat and waited till 4.44 a.m. In the meantime, I read the holy book, chanted, and acupressure.

At 4.44 a.m. as I began to meditate, I saw Lord Buddha smiling at me. He was above the Sahasrara, pouring energy in the form of white light to the Sahasrara. The energy passed through all my chakras. After a while, I saw him coming and sitting next to me.

He told me to accept a leaf from the Bodhi tree. He said it's the tree where he attained enlightenment. He placed the leaf in my hand. It appeared as a peepal leaf, very fresh and green. He said, "I want you to visit the place."

He then took me along to the place where he attained enlightenment and made me sit in the same place where he sat. I could see myself blue in colour. My aura was radiating white light. After a while, he brought me back, and blessed me. I thanked him for his blessings. He then left. A member from our meditation group called up later and told me it was Buddha Purnima. I told her, "I didn't know. I have only one calendar at home, the one Guruji gave us at our Visakhapatnam retreat. It has no festivals marked."

Lord Budha's statue became live

During one of my evening meditations, I saw Lord Buddha's black statue in a standing position. From nowhere, a beautiful cream-coloured drape began to dress him. The drape gracefully went over his shoulders. Suddenly, the statue became live to his original form. He smiled and lifted one hand, and sent his blessings to me. He then slowly sat down with his legs folded and began meditating.

Lord Buddha Came Home

One day, during meditation, I was guided to bring home Lord Buddha. He appeared and told me to bring him home before 12 a.m. He wished to be permanently in my house. Soon I received a call from a friend. After disconnecting the call, a photo of Lord Buddha flashed on my mobile and stayed. I immediately took a screenshot. This was really strange. I don't have any pictures of Buddha on my phone or at home. How could a picture of Lord Buddha appear on the screen? After this, every few minutes, Buddha's idol kept flashing in front of my eyes. This kept on till late evening. I shared my experience with a member of our meditation group, how repeatedly I am being guided to buy a statue or painting and was shown it has to be bought and brought inside the house before 12 a.m.

She told me, "Hold on, Sruthi, let me check, what's it tomorrow." Happily, she came back and said, "Tomorrow is Buddha Purnima. Please go and buy it. It is an indication. Lord Buddha is finally coming home. Those in meditation do have Buddha's statues at home. Even I have one; Guruji had given me. In your case, it's different, he has been wanting to come to your house from a very long time."

Same time, my friend...the one whom I have earlier shared about, (who has travelled with me to various places, after I had visions from my teens) happened to call me up. I answered her call and told her, "I need to go out to buy a Buddha idol or painting as shown in meditation, I will call back." Hearing about Buddha, she requested me to share my meditation experiences with her as she was curious. I shared my experience and also told her about Lord Buddha's wish to come home since a long time. She is a Buddhist and is into Vipassana meditation but never spoke on spirituality.

On hearing me, she said, "Please keep the phone and go. Get the idol immediately. Your meditation experience is very auspicious. Buddha wants to be in your house before 12 a.m. It has great significance. Tomorrow is Buddha Purnima; the day Buddha was born."

She requested me to share something more about Lord Buddha. I told her, "Last year, I have been there in meditation. Lord Buddha himself took me there and made me sit at the exact place where he attained enlightenment. I am sharing this in short. Later on, I came to know it was Buddha Purnima."

While she was talking, a shop was shown to me where I could get the statue. Now I was sure I had to get Lord Buddha home.

I told her, "I will bring him home today."

I went to the particular shop shown to me. The shopkeeper showed me two statues; one was very good. Its vibe was welcoming. I was guided to buy the first idol.

Seeing the photo, the member of our meditation group, who told me about Buddha Poornima, said, "It doesn't look like the normal statues. It is special, very peaceful, and positive looks; It has something special to it." She was aware that Lord Buddha wanted to come home since a few years.

The shopkeeper reduced the cost on his own and asked me, "Do you want a lamp?". I said, "No". He selected a lovely brass lamp, saying, "This is the latest design. Take it." It looked very nice. I asked him, "How much do I have to pay?" He said, "No cost." He guided me on a few things. After coming home, I was shown where to place the idol of Lord Buddha.

Just after placing the idol within a few minutes the energy in the idol could be felt. It was radiating brightness. Lord Buddha's presence is there in the idol. The statue is divine, the same as Lord Krishna's.

Before this, I had never ever bought or had a statue, painting, or photo of Lord Buddha.

My Sacred Experiences with Goddesses

Goddess Kali

I saw a Goddess and was guided she was Goddess Kali. She was dark-skinned, (dark shade of blue), had red eyes, and her tongue sticking out. She had worn a garland of skulls. She seemed very powerful and angry and was killing a demon. After killing the demon, she kept her leg on Lord Shiva, she then became calm, looked at me, and smiled. She blessed me. A lemon came out from her hand, it rolled and came to me.

Maa Kurathiamma happily comes towards the Temple

During a morning meditation, I saw Maa Kurathiamma. First, I could only see eyes. Then, I saw her dressed as a village girl, happily walking and coming towards the temple. She was playfully keeping her legs criss-cross, as the Bharat Natyam dancers walk while performing a dance.

She entered the temple and smiled at me. She kept walking, entered the sanctum, and merged into the idol. I got up and went to see her. She smiled through the idol.

Goddess on a Tiger

Once, during my meditation, a Goddess appeared on a tiger. She was enclosed in a very bright and strong aura. She looked very powerful. From her right hand, she kept sending divine energy to me.

Durga Maa enclosed me in her aura

Towards the end of a morning meditation, I saw too much brightness. Through the brightness, I could see a Goddess appearing slowly.

She was sitting on a lion and she had many hands holding different articles: Trishul, conch, sword, lotus, and many more. She gave me blessings. Her aura was very bright and powerful, and Divine light shone on me. She enclosed me in her aura.

Maa Kurathiamma calling me

Maa Kurathiamma wanted me to seek her blessings, and I went there in meditation.

I received Maa Kurathiamma's and Gurus' room darshan and blessings.

Maa Kurathiamma smiling at me through her idol

Once, during morning meditation, I saw an old, closed, brown, wooden door. Soon, the door opened, and I could see Maa Kurathiamma's idol. She was smiling at me through the idol. I received her blessings. She has appeared and blessed me many times.

Goddess Bhawani's idol became live and blessed me

One day morning, while meditating, I could see a temple with a wooden door wide open. There was an idol of a Goddess.

She had worn a dark green saree with gold motifs and a gold saree border, green and gold bangles, a deep red round bindi of red vermillion, and had multiple hands with different articles, one of them was a sword. She also had worn layers of necklaces, one necklace having the shape of coins. Her long hair was left open. She became live and blessed me. I was shown that she is Goddess Bhawani. I haven't heard much about her. Instantly, I was guided that she is a form of Goddess Durga or Parvati. I had earlier received their blessings.

I had a very beautiful and divine experience with Maa Kali a year back.

Goddess Shakambhari

Earlier, just the name Shakambhari was repeatedly shown to me in visions. As this name was unique, I remember sharing this name with my house help's kid. He memorized it and repeated it.

Some years later, I received her blessings during my initial days of meditation. She used to repeatedly appear during meditation and let me know she is around me protecting me.

Later on, during an evening meditation, I received the blessings of Goddess Shakambhari. She appeared with lots of fruits and vegetables, a lotus in one hand, and a bow in the other hand. Same day, the temple where she resides was shown to me.

Goddess Lakshmi & Saraswati

I saw two Goddesses. One of them was sitting on a pink lotus. There were coins falling out from her hand, and some fell and came near me. The second Goddess was dressed in white and she had a musical instrument in her hand. Both of them seemed happy and they showered blessings on me.

Goddess Lalita

I received the darshan and blessings of Goddess Lalita during meditation. My meditation experience with Goddess Lalita was divine. I haven't heard or read about her before.

Goddess Chandraghanta

Once when I got up, I received an insight to meditate at 4.44 a.m. I posted my pranams at 4.44 a.m. in our meditation group and began meditating. After a while into meditation, I could see a white lotus. Soon, a Goddess appeared in a dark blue background. Her third eye was open and she had eight hands holding different articles, the name Chandraghanta was shown to me. I have never heard this name ever. She blessed me with divine energy, stayed for a few seconds, and slowly vanished.

After going through my post on the above experience, a member of our meditation group shared a few details on Goddess Chandraghanta as follows: "Goddess Chandraghanta is also known as Chandika, she is the form of Goddess Durga. Her third eye is always open, signifying her readiness for battle against evil. She is believed to reward people with her grace, bravery, and courage. By her virtue, all the sins, distresses, physical sufferings, mental tribulations, and ghostly hurdles of the devotees are eradicated. I remember that in Kerala, there is a special havan (a revered fire ceremony in Hinduism) conducted known as the Chandika Homam."

Lady of Lourdes, France

While meditating, I saw a grotto with a statue of Mother Mary holding the Holy Rosary and smiling at me. The name "Lady of Lourdes" was shown to me. After meditation, I could recollect seeing the grotto in one of the photos a nun shared with me almost seven years ago, on her visit to France, to 'Our Lady of Lourdes.'

I also remembered how the nun told me that during her visit, one night she couldn't sleep at all. Mother Mary appeared to her and guided her to buy me a souvenir- Mother Mary's statue and a rosary. She told her to get it blessed and hand it over to me as soon as she reached Mumbai from France.

The nun had called me on WhatsApp from France and told me the guidance she received. She added that it is Mother Mary's wish and that she is buying something for me. She requested me to meet her the day she reached Mumbai.

On reaching Mumbai, she came over to a convent near my place and handed over a small silver statue of 'Our Lady of Lourdes' and a beautiful silver rosary to me. She told me it was miraculous and blessed, and asked me to keep it safe. I happily thanked her for her goodness and narrated how I had received Mother Mary's blessings earlier too and how, from an early age, my life was full of miracles.

On hearing this, she phoned her brother, who is a priest. He expressed his wish to meet me and hear more. Later, I met him along with my mom.

Healing Others After Initiation

I have never asked Guruji how to heal anyone, but healing came to me naturally, after receiving guidance from nature. After a few years of healing many people, Guruji told me, "Very good. You need not worry; nothing will affect you. You have done a lot of healing for free; many are ungrateful. From now on, you must charge for healing."

I was silent hearing Guruji say these words. Guruji strictly repeated, "Don't heal anyone for free, else they will not get a complete benefit."

I have never met anyone I healed. When someone messages or calls me for healing, while reading the message, I get an insight or my sixth sense that guides me on whether the person should be helped or not. I channel energy instantly with a thought, and people benefit immediately.

At times, I am guided that I should stay away from healing some people. In some cases, the energy doesn't go, and it comes back. Guruji had told me, "All may not be able to reach you"

Earlier I used to help everyone. Now, I strictly follow Guruji's guidance. He told me, "Only the good will benefit. Try to heal only the good people." One should heal only if they are healthy and guided to heal. If one's energy levels are low, it is advisable not to heal others. Some diseases can sap the maximum energy.

I have healed many people from various serious conditions, including diabetes, lung cancer, breast cancer, leukaemia, TB, depression, dangerously low platelet counts, low haemoglobin, very low vitamin D levels (one of our meditation group ex-member's vitamin D level rose from 5 to 12 in a week), low B12, high ESR, heart issues, rheumatoid arthritis, fluctuating blood pressure, kidney problems, and severe pain, non-stop bleeding of several months, severe liver issues, among others.

Experience of a member of our meditation group – As narrated by her

On 04/02/2019, I was on the verge of losing my life, I could feel I was leaving, so I messaged Guruji (with great difficulty, as I was not able to hold the mobile, I placed the mobile on a nearby pillow so that I could avoid holding it to type) that I had no stamina to even stand or move on my own. There was no one around me. After sometime, Guruji called me up and told me to reach out to emergency service.

I somehow arranged for my office emergency service with the help of one of my colleagues. My colleague told me to try to keep the door open so that the emergency service people could enter my house. I told her I had no stamina to reach the door and would see what to do when they arrived.

Guruji put a message in our KMG group, informing our members to help. Some of our dear members got ready to reach my home and informed me that they were on the way.

Seeing his message in the group, Sruthi immediately gave me a call. She said, "Should I come over?", I told her, "No, I don't want to trouble you. Some of our meditation group members are coming." She lovingly continued, "Do self-healing for your uterus. I will pass energy to you, but you do self-healing".

I told her in a low voice (I had no strength to talk), "Sruthi, I have no strength. I tried placing my palms on my uterus, but they did not remain there. My palms are falling down on their own, and I am not able to hold for even a few seconds." She said with a concerned voice, "You try now. Keep trying. I am keeping the phone, you try, you can do it", Saying this, she kept the phone.

I felt to give it a last try and I could see I was able to do self-healing. Within a few seconds of doing self-healing, I felt a gush of energy at my lower back, with tingling around, and I was just alright. By the time the emergency service reached my society gate, I was all normal. I had to tell them, "One of my friends is arranging to take me to the hospital."

By the time some of our meditation group members reached my home after seeing Guruji's message in the group, I had gained strength from the healing energy passed by Sruthi and could move around, open the door for them, and welcome them. Some of them insisted they take me to hospital, but I was not feeling sick at all. Only after making sure there was someone near me, my office emergency team left.

I thanked Guruji and our group members. I had forgotten what exactly happened on that day. Recently, in my meditation, I got clear insight of the sequence of the incidents and how I received the gush of energy from Sruthi at my lower back, and I was full of energy all of a sudden.

Healing People With Coronavirus

With Guruji's grace and blessings, I started healing and guiding a few of our meditation group members.

I had the opportunity to heal several people suffering from Coronavirus, with the first being a relative of a member of our meditation group. I performed the healing by viewing her pictures and videos. At that time, Guruji had not yet specifically instructed me not to heal individuals with Coronavirus.

Very High Fever

Once, a close family friend reached out to me about her brother, who was suffering from a high fever. She mentioned that his temperature was 104.8°F and had confirmed it using three different devices: an oral thermometer, a digital thermometer, and an infrared thermometer, all showing the same reading. I could tell it was a serious situation.

Upon seeing him, I was sure he would be fine soon, I immediately gave him a blood-cleaning. I noticed his pulse was quite elevated and his body seemed to lack resistance.

As I channelled healing energy, I could feel it flowed rapidly from me to him, and he was able to absorb it effortlessly.

Within a minute of healing, I felt his pulse stabilized, and his fever dropped from 104.8°F to 100.1°F and then to 99.5°F. And then, within 2-3 minutes, his temperature returned to normal.

Healing A Wounded Dog

During the lockdown, my previous flat's neighbour aunty asked for help. I had healed her dog of high fever earlier. Her dog was having an ear infection, and blood was coming out of his ears due to injury by scratching.

Due to COVID-19, she feared to take her pet to the vet. I gave him healing, and he instantly went into deep sleep. The same evening, without any medication, his ear infection was cleared, and the injury was healed.

That same evening, aunty called me, her voice filled with amazement and relief. Without any medication, the dog's ear infection had cleared and the injury from scratching had healed. She expressed her heartfelt gratitude, overwhelmed by the swift and complete recovery of her beloved pet.

My guidance to meditation group members

In 2020, I started guiding two of our meditation group members. They started following the teachings, were having juices, and meditating twice daily. One of them messaged me, saying that her sadness had disappeared, her thoughts of leaving the world too had disappeared, and that she was happy and peaceful. The other member also mentioned being happy. Guruji was extremely happy when he came to know I had helped members who were struggling to find peace and happiness since years. He blessed me.

Another member of our meditation group, messaged me, saying that with my healing, she is in the best of health.

Then on, I healed and guided a group member's aunt, another group member's husband, and many more members.

A member of our meditation group had been struggling to have Anar juice for many years. He was guided by Guruji quite a few times, but he was unable to follow. He said, "Some or the other obstacle comes, and I cannot complete what Guruji said. This has been going on for years." During our Mysore Retreat, Guruji strictly told him to consume Anar juice for specific days. He was worried and sought my help. I channelled energy after receiving an insight to help him. I told him it would be done, be positive. During our Guru Poornima function in Hyderabad, he told me, "I completed specific days of Anar juice that Guruji instructed. It was possible with your blessings." In gratitude, he offered his pranams to me. I smiled and told him, "You should have informed me earlier. I knew the day you had completed it."

Another member of our meditation group had written to me, seeking help on diabetes. His diabetes on a daily basis was 250-300. His body couldn't naturally produce insulin. I sent him healing energy and channelled things silently so that he would bring a change in his diet. I didn't write or reply to him, but I could see his progress.

Two days before our Guru Poornima function, I felt like asking him about his progress but then thought it would be good to ask him face to face and see his reaction. I met him and asked, "How are you doing?" He happily told me his diabetes is now between 150-200, and he is following a specific diet schedule. I told him to carry on and also follow Guruji's Instructions. He seemed very happy.

They all thanked me for the healing.

Sruthi Saving my schizophrenic husband from suicide – As Narrated by a meditation group member:

When the lockdown came, due to fear of stepping out to buy things, we both didn't follow Guruji's instructions properly for a few months. This caused major faults in our system, and we both fell very badly sick. Though I was talking to Sruthi at that time, she was not guiding me then. Soon Guruji put me under Her guidance

Sruthi also told me that my husband is not mad, that his symptoms were of schizophrenia, and advised consulting a doctor. He was suicidal. Sruthi kept healing him from a distance, and he came out of his suicidal tendencies. I soon found a good doctor who put him on medication.

Soon after the lockdown, she asked me to get some tests done for both of us. When I shared my test reports with Guruji, He replied, "The report shows you are going to suffer and die". I shared my reports with Sruthi, she told me, "I will help you with one condition; you need to follow Guruji's instructions strictly."

We started following everything. Sruthi sent healing to my husband and me. She kept sending healing to both of us whenever needed. Slowly, we started having changes in our bodies and energy levels. Slowly, my husband's diabetes (which was my long-lasted worry) began to come under control.

Before Guruji put me under Sruthi's guidance, my fears had consumed me, I was completely in a lost state, there was no confidence, and I couldn't use my brain properly. Same time ego was the biggest hindrance to progress. It was impossible to bring change in me the way Sruthi did, with the state I was in. With her guidance, things started changing for the best. Guruji putting me under her guidance was the biggest turning point of my life.

Avoiding a Heart attack

A family friend was in poor health, with dangerously low heartbeats confirmed by an ECG as a condition called Bradycardia. The doctor advised him to immediately do two blood tests to find out if he was on the verge of a heart attack.

He did the tests, called me, and told me the above matter. Immediately, I sent him healing and told him to repeat an ECG after a while. I also told him, "Don't worry your reports will be good. You will be fine. Meet your doctor in the morning with your ECG and blood test reports."

He repeated the ECG. His ECG report was normal, and the blood test reports came the next morning. They were normal. The doctor was surprised to see the reports and said, "There's nothing to worry. Everything is fine"

Warding Off Negative Energies

I once asked Guruji how to ward off negative energies if absorbed. I inquired because many members of our meditation group were seeking guidance on this.

With a smile, Guruji replied, "You go to sleep after healing; I do the same."

I mentioned to him that I had been following this practice.

An ex-member's Recovery

In Dec 2021, I saw Sruthi bringing back our meditation group's ex-member to life right in front of my eyes within a few minutes after she collapsed.

We had decided to meet for a task given to us by Guruji. By the time Sruthi and I reached the restaurant, we saw our meditation group's ex-member had collapsed. Her head was placed on her hand on top of the table, she was making sounds, her eyes were shut. She was sweating profusely right in front of the chilled AC. Her clothes were drenched due to heavy sweating, her palms were very cold. The waiters and floor manager were seen worried and requested us to rush her to the hospital.

They were ready to call for an ambulance. At that time, Sruthi said, "Give me one minute".

Sruthi checked her pulse, and there was almost no pulse, and by then the sounds she was making stopped altogether. Sruthi kept giving healing energy to her, and within a minute or two she opened her eyes, and Sruthi gave her water to drink.

After drinking that water, a glow came on her face, and she became normal within a few minutes. Everyone at the restaurant was witness to what had happened: the waiters, the floor manager, and everyone were relieved.

Flight Experience of a member of our meditation group - As narrated by her

On April 2nd, 2023, filled with full of energy, positivity, and joy, I arrived early at Mumbai airport. Before boarding, I received compliments from fellow group members on my looks and my cheerful demeanour. Our seats, 22F for me and 23A for Sruthi, weren't together.

Sruthi called me and said, "Do you want to swap your seat? The guy sitting next to me is happy to swap the seat, as he is sitting between us two women; he looked uncomfortable." I immediately said, "yes". Unknowingly at that very moment, my life-saving journey began.

As the flight took off, I happily conversed with Sruthi. Thirty minutes in the air, the hostess served us plain pulao, which I accepted as Prasad. I told Sruthi, "See, it is falling under Guruji's protocols, I am hungry, and it came at the right time." Saying this I started having the food while it was hot, taking care not to drop even a single bit of it. After a while, Sruthi took a spoon of the food and told me, "The food is not ok; it's not prepared the right way". I had almost finished my food by then. Soon after, the announcement of our landing came. I told Sruthi, "I feel some discomfort, but nothing severe."

We exchanged some light talk, and soon the flight started to land, we both closed our ears and prepared ourselves for the landing. After a few minutes, in mid-air, I felt the area we were at, wasn't good, I felt highly negative. Suddenly I felt heavy jerks in the flight; it kept increasing, the landing was not happening and my discomfort increased instantly, I tried to tell Sruthi, saw her eyes and ears closed, and I couldn't get my voice out. I felt not to disturb her, too. I kept praying, "Please hit the ground; it's more than enough."

I tried to open my eyes to see if we were near the ground, but I couldn't. By the time the flight finally landed, I felt completely drained of energy.

I unlocked the food tray in front of me, placed my head on it, and collapsed. Sruthi called out my name, but I couldn't respond, though I could hear her. She tapped me, but I could not say anything.

And then I had my first out-of-body experience, seeing myself on the chair with my legs splayed out. Sruthi was continuously healing me, and I felt I would come back. We had landed by now. As people started disembarking, Sruthi asked, "Are you okay? Your pulse is low; do you feel anything?"

She lifted my hand to check the pulse. After a minute or so, my hand kept falling as if I had no life (she later told me my body temperature was going down). She checked my BP; it was 67 - 45, pulse was 54. Sruthi kept tapping me to stop me from falling into a deep sleep. Even after everyone had disembarked, I couldn't move an inch. I felt that I should attempt to get up, but I couldn't. She continued healing me, assuring me I would be okay and not to give up. Sruthi called out for help, and the flight attendants gathered around. They too checked my BP and panicked, and they called for help at the airport. I wanted to vomit, but couldn't. They discussed arranging a wheelchair and emergency services, and soon, a wheelchair was arranged.

Unable to respond, my eyes remained closed after feeling completely drained. Sruthi, using her healing touch, told me, "Try getting up now and sit in the wheelchair."

After she said this, I could move. Slowly, I dragged my body towards the wheelchair and sat on it. Soon, my eyes closed again, and my head dropped to the right side; I couldn't hold it up.

Sruthi pumped energy into me, and I felt my soul moving between two realms, in and out of my body (this stabilized, and my soul remained in my body only after she healed me in the cab later). The airport staff rushed me from the flight and ran towards the airport. The staff brought me to another part of the airport. I searched for Sruthi, eyes still closed, thinking, "Where is Sruthi? Did they make her run? They should not make her run." Then the speed increased again, and they took me near the conveyor belt.

I could hear Sruthi and felt relieved. Someone mentioned Electral, but I didn't get any. I saw a cookie being offered, but I couldn't eat it; I signalled no and couldn't sip water.

I was rushed to a small emergency room. There I opened my eyes and searched for a bed, as I wanted to lay down for a while, but found no bed inside that small room, I couldn't keep my eyes open for long, so closed them, my head was dropping throughout my time in the wheelchair. I felt a touch on my Sahasrara; my uneasiness increased. I signalled those around me for no touch with my eyes still closed. I could hear a couple of members of our meditation group, but couldn't respond.

After a while, I heard Sruthi asking the doctor about my condition, and he said my blood pressure was dangerously low that without hospitalization, I would 100% slip into a coma, and that I needed an IV. He advised rushing me to a hospital emergency unit immediately, as Udaipur airport had no facilities.

Sruthi asked if he could arrange a vehicle, as she didn't want to leave me alone.

A fellow meditation group member told Sruthi to take the Innova, and she instantly agreed. The helper took my wheelchair near the car while the other members looked on. The member asked Sruthi to inform her which hospital I would be taken to, and Sruthi agreed. No member of our meditation group accompanied me; Sruthi managed everything on her own, reassuring me that nothing would happen to me.

I collapsed onto the back seat of the Innova and wanted to sleep. Sruthi, carrying bags, got into the front seat with the driver. She took me to the first hospital, but it was closed, as was the second hospital. The driver, who had another pickup, kindly offered to arrange another vehicle instead of leaving us stranded. On the way, Sruthi encouraged me to vomit, saying I would feel better. After she said this, I instantly vomited, feeling a little better and able to speak (here my soul started remaining in my body). She messaged Guruji that I was much better, and he sent his blessings.

Sruthi joined me in the back seat and healed me again. The driver reassured me, but with Sruthi near, I told him I wasn't afraid; I just felt like lying down. When we reached the third hospital, which was also closed due to a strike, I vomited again and felt much better. Sruthi suggested we go to the resort instead, and I agreed.

At the resort entry, two members of our meditation group approached us, offering medication. I declined, wanting to vomit again. The hotel staff quickly arranged a wheelchair, and I was taken to our room, which had a bad odour. Sruthi joined me and gave me more healing, normalizing my blood pressure to 107/62 and my pulse to 89, a first for me (My BP used to be low for years, and it had dropped further upon this incident). Guruji too declared I was all alright. I bounced back in full swing within a few hours of Sruthi's healing. I could go to the loo and after that, I got my appetite back, I could have lemon water and eat food. Earlier I couldn't sense anything about a place, Sruthi had helped me to open my senses so that I could sense the places which were not good, I felt happy that I could for the first time sense negativity of places.

After returning to Mumbai, several doctors, unrelated to each other, all denied the need for an IV for me. One doctor even took my ECG, which was normal, and confirmed there was no problem. He asked if I felt like fainting once a month, I said no, I only faint when something gets triggered once in a while

He asked, "How much can you walk?" I told him, "I can easily walk for an hour without any trouble."

He told me, "Then I don't recommend any treatment for you, as there is nothing wrong with you. Have confidence".

I got my haemoglobin test, lung function test, and liver function tests done, all results came normal.

Here I repeat Guruji's words: "When Sruthi is there with you, there is no need to worry."

Multiple miracles By Sruthi - As narrated by a member of our meditation group

I wasn't able to sense, taste, or smell anything. I couldn't make out if a dish was good, bad, or spoilt; I used to just eat to fill my stomach.

Once, after multiple instances of vomiting and bowel movements, I sought help in our meditation group and recalled having eaten possibly spoiled boiled eggs.

After receiving healing from Sruthi, I gradually began to sense the taste of food items and could roughly identify their ingredients by smell. Now, I thoroughly enjoy my meals.

Sruthi also silently healed my father on several occasions. Since my parents couldn't follow Guruji's protocols, she advised me that my father might need to see a doctor for his extremely high blood pressure. My father who was against medicines and doctors, now religiously gets his BP checked and takes medicines. I have never seen him visit a doctor earlier. My mother says it is a miracle.

Concerned about my parents living alone, I shared this with Sruthi. She asked if any of my siblings lived close by, and I mentioned my brother, who was working and staying nearby. She assured me that they would get help, and that same day, my brother informed me that his company had granted him permanent work-from-home status and he could come to live with our parents. I joyfully shared this news with Sruthi, who remarked that he is a nice person. I felt relieved knowing my brother could now be available whenever needed.

Sruthi channels energy and continues to create remarkable miracles in my life and in the lives of my loved ones. Her silent work touches many people, bringing about positive transformations time and again.

Reversing Diabetes & Other Ailments

As narrated by a member of the meditation group:

With Sruthi's healing, my husband's latest HbA1C test results showed a reading of 6.1, indicating pre-diabetes (the pre-diabetic range is 5.7-6.4). This was unimaginable for me and was impossible for me to even think of.

Before coming under Sruthi's guidance, his diabetes was a cause of worry for me for almost 20 years, with lots of nightmares. At times, his blood sugar levels skyrocketed to over 400, and after turning 40, his fasting sugar levels never dropped below 250, even with medication from experienced doctors. His HbA1C was consistently above 9, and doctors advised him to cut down on food. When we followed their guidance, his weight plummeted suddenly, and his nervous system weakened.

With such high diabetes, his sleep was often disturbed with body pains. He would sweat profusely, sometimes so much that the sweat would drop from his body like flowing water. He would feel excessive heat and would pour water over himself in the midnight. I would worry and remained stressed, not knowing what to do. He frequently ate out, adding to my concerns. I prayed all those years for an effective solution for his diabetes, and my prayers were answered through Sruthi.

After coming under her guidance, she advised me on which foods to avoid and reassured me, saying, "Friend, your expectations are too high; it will delay the healing process. His sugar levels will come down; have patience."

After she started helping him, his HbA1C gradually dropped from 9 to 7.8, then to 6.7, and now to a pre-diabetic level of 6.1, which is excellent for someone with a long history of diabetes. He began enjoying healthy meals and became a pre-diabetic too. Even after regularly consuming sweet dishes made out of jaggery, his sugar levels would remain within the normal range. I monitored his sugar levels at home and kept a chart. Remarkably, his latest test was conducted after a few days of consuming jaggery sweets.

He was a diabetic and had been on insulin for three years. Seeing his report, he joked, "Now I can have 1 kg of sweets." He became peaceful, started singing songs, enjoying his sleep, and no longer complained about any pain. This is really a miracle.

Despite being diabetic, and months after receiving Sruthi's healing, he kept eating unwanted things as he is a foodie, which slowly worsened his condition and increased his WBC count. After seeing the reports, Sruthi advised me to consult a good MD and follow the instructions. The MD recommended further tests, which I informed Sruthi about. She sent healings to my husband and assured me that the reports would be normal. The CT scan and other blood tests were normal.

However, due to my husband's high WBC count, the MD referred him to a haematologist. Seeing my husband's reports, the haematologist was sure that he was into chronic leukaemia. We got the tests done, and I prayed to Sruthi to heal my husband of CLL while awaiting the results for three days, which were the toughest days of my life. The results came normal. By the time the results came, Sruthi had healed him from a distance. She instructed me to happily inform the doctor of the normal results. The doctor was shocked and said, "Yes I was waiting for this report. I already got a copy; we are happy about the results. There is no danger now; you can continue treatment of the MD."

He said that he asked to get the blood test done for leukaemia because of the chances of CLL indicated in the WBC count. I thanked him and left, feeling immensely grateful.

A Miracle Recovery: Saving a Life After a Tragic Accident

Sometime back, my maid's husband experienced a life-threatening accident. After dropping their son at school, he was hit by a garbage truck whose driver, who was drunk, lost control. Thrown off the road, he suffered severe head injuries, bleeding from his ears, and a dislocated arm with a fractured shoulder. Bystanders helped, noted the truck's number, and stopped the driver.

That night, my maid, who is very close to me, called in distress, explaining his critical condition and their inability to afford treatment. I reassured her, channelled energy, and told her he would soon regain consciousness and stabilize before his CT scan. Miraculously, he regained consciousness without pain, and the scan showed no head trauma. However, doctors insisted that surgery costing over ₹2.5 lakhs was necessary to restore his arm's function.

Days later, when she brought him home, I visited her, offered assistance, and channelled healing energy. Her husband's health gradually improved. Later, during his final X-ray, the doctors were shocked to see that his arm had healed naturally, with major bones and joints aligning perfectly, without surgery or plaster.

The doctors called it a rare and miraculous case. Despite the severity of the accident, he recovered fully, a testament to the grace and healing energy that restored him to normalcy.

Words from Those Touched by My Journey

Testimonial

Sruthi, you have such Divine Darshans but the one that I felt most peaceful reading is this one. I find Lord Narasimha is the most fascinating of all Avatars. How it must have felt to behold the glorious form is simply beyond my imagination. If just visualising can be so enchanting what it must be to see the Lord. Sages and others perform penance for years and here the Lord appears before you out of love for your pure devotion. Please keep sharing. Even reading can bestow inexplicable joy.

Testimonial

Sruthi, I remember lots of instances and I witnessed lots of instances where you have been brilliantly healing many people, animals, and plants and even calming down many of the natural calamities, or disrupts.

I was very enthusiastic to be a healer, after learning Reiki I tried healing many people, before meeting our Guruji. After meeting Guruji, soon my desire to become a healer manifolded in me strongly.

I went through my entire chat with you and found the first time you sent me healing was on 1st April 2018 while talking to you I had mentioned severe back pain, at 11:11 am you sent me healing energy, and at 11:13 am the pain disappeared with no efforts from me after telling You.

Testimonial

A couple of days back I wanted to get some important documents from my personal laptop, but the laptop was not in use for a few years. It didn't open, I tried several techniques, but it didn't open, I prayed to Sruthi, and instantly it opened and I could get my documents on time. I remember Guruji telling me, "You can pray to Sruthi. She has reached that level, but it should come from the heart."

From my experience, it should come from 100% acceptance. Prayers work wonders when there is acceptance. When one has acceptance, one won't shy away or think even a fraction of a seconds to appreciate the help we receive, the joy of it spills out automatically. I have heard a grateful life is the only meaningful life, at the end, the rest of the things don't even matter. When we are grateful, every moment of our life is taken care of, and gratitude spills out directly from the heart in different forms of expression of appreciation, one has no control to hold it back. True happiness is in gratitude, it brings that smile which never fades away.

Guruji personally explained to me the meaning of gratitude. His eyes were full of love towards Sruthi and his eyes were wet. At that moment, I realised my mistake. I was a highly egoistic person. I would wonder why Guruji put me under Sruthi's guidance. Only after he put me under Sruthi's guidance, changes began in me, with her tremendous efforts and kindness.

Today, I understand, why he put me under her guidance, it was to help me, break my ego, and to bring a tremendous positive change in me. I have noticed the communication between our Poojya Guruji and Sruthi, they need not talk and can communicate through eyes.

Testimonial

Poojya Guruji with your blessings and Sruthi's unending love and guidance, I am experiencing real peace, joy and I am spreading smiles and happiness to everyone, I come across ☺☺ ☺☺

When one is under a powerful Guru, not only she or he, but his or her family starts receiving tremendous blessings from the Guru, it is a process of uplifting many lives, and a powerful Guru takes as his or her responsibility. Many of our meditation group members might have met my cousin at the Kannur retreat, I had introduced him to Sruthi. His jobless state was creating a lot of disturbances between his parents and him. I had shared with Sruthi my wish of decades that my uncle (my cousin's father) and family get good financial support, and she answered my prayer. She assured me he would get a good job abroad. I am happy beyond words as my cousin has secured a govt job in Dubai, within a short period of time, and with no hassles, he went abroad with the help of Sruthi. My entire family is happy that my cousin securing a good job. It was my grandmother's wish to see him in a secure job and the way he got the govt job in Dubai miraculously is impossible in today's Era and unexplainable. My entire family is happy and rejoicing

Testimonial

After being guided by Sruthi, my impulsiveness disappeared, I started enjoying every moment of life, I started reflecting deeply before responding, and I could feel inner peace. She taught me to be myself and guided me to spread love, peace, kindness, and happiness wherever I go and I am trying my best to do the same. She told me "I want to see you spreading kindness wherever you go".

Testimonial

In Guruji's healing room, he was sitting and listening to me. The moment I began to offer him gratitude, he swiftly stood up, held my arms, and took me towards Sruthi.

Guruji told me, "Thank her, she is the one who helped you. When Sruthi is there with you, there is no need to worry."

Poojya Guruji, like my earlier Gurus, did not take any credit, which truly shows their purity and selflessness.

Testimonial

Shruti has always been my inspiration of soul consciousness. Whenever I felt loneliness, I thought of Shruti and would become quiet. She hugged me in Hyderabad Guru Purnima and I felt instantly energized. Guruji had specifically asked me to come on the day you were to come to his home. He wanted me to meet you. You showed me self-healing with love and faith and after that, I really started self-healing.

Testimonial

I had sought Shrutis help for healing my earlier cook. She has been having Rheumatoid Arthritis and was taking two painkillers a day to sustain. I met her in Mumbai and somehow Shruti appeared in my awareness and I sought her help. The next day itself my cook reported that she had no pain and did not take any painkillers. This has been so far. Immense Gratitude Sruthi for your Healing.

Testimonial

I bow down to you, Shruti. We are blessed, dear. With Your real experiences, we too get a glimpse of the different cosmic world as if you take all of us, there, to see and experience the divinity. Just by reading, we feel blissful, I can't even imagine, how blissful you must be. Your every experience is divine.

Testimonial

Dear Shruti, thank you so much for posting. I find your posts so valuable and heartfelt. They are awe-inspiring and motivational in every sense. From my experience, I have derived tremendous strength from your sharing.

In my life, I have seen too many ups and downs. I have been misunderstood, betrayed by my own people, and condemned for things that were not my fault. I've suffered injuries, accidents, illnesses, failures, and lots more, to the point where I had given up hope and was very isolated.

Few friends during those phases of life, who eventually deserted me at a crucial juncture in my life for their selfish reasons, but at the time used to sympathize and feel overwhelmed about how my life is inexplicably and traumatically unbelievable. When challenges in my life wouldn't cease and perhaps became too much for them to handle, they parted ways for greener pastures. May they stay blessed always!

However, there was almost no one that I knew, who could have related to my life as a whole and understood its twists and turns, as a result of which I could never find anyone to share my complete story. Only someone who has seen such depths would understand what I am saying. That someone was you., Sruthi.

Since a few months I have been staying alone and I have realised it's not easy. Many times, I discuss with my mother- that we sit in the comforts of our house and read your messages. But believe me, even if I had to go through half of your struggles, I would have been dead long back!

Testimonial

Eight months back when I shifted to Mumbai, due to ignorance, I landed in a miserable house. There were continuous fights in my building sometimes till 12 in the night. There were a lot of water problems. Sometimes we did not have a drop of water for 2-3 days. I was getting worried as I had taken a very large decision to leave my house and I did not want it to fail.

I messaged Shruti to help me find a new house where I could live peacefully.

The broker took me to a beautiful house. I just loved it. In the evening, I thought I should go in search with some other broker too as I did not want to land in any more trouble. One of my son's friend's mother referred me to the other broker. He also took me to the same beautiful house. Both the brokers showed me around 15 to 20 houses each but both started with the same beautiful house. The house was the perfect house I was looking for. I finally said yes to that house although the rent was a little more. Then I came to know that someone else was taking that house. Finally, after few days the broker contacted me again saying that the deal was cancelled and I got my present house. I am still in the same house, very comfortable.

Shruti was a large saviour for me. Thanks, dear for all the help.

Testimonial

Shruti...reading every message and experience of yours brings so much hope and confidence in life. I would love to connect with you and learn more from you.

Testimonial

Thank you for sharing your experiences with us, Shruti. It is divine and powerful to hear how you got through those tremendously difficult stages in life. Your sharing and willpower keep us motivated. It is a great learning for us.

Testimonial

Your joy is so palpable, Shruti. I still remember the emotion you conveyed when you spoke at the retreat. Your shining smile and happiness are one to be cherished. Through patience, grit, courage, and suffering, Shruti, you are a marvellous example of showing strength, positivity, and determination in the face of the mountain you conquered. You are a medical miracle.

Testimonial

Sruthi, thank you very much for sharing real mind-blowing experiences. You were fearless since childhood. I realise, there are lots of life lessons to learn from your experiences. For those who are good at observing, absorbing, and accepting there are so many lessons to learn from your experiences, when I go through your experiences, I feel like reading epics.

In childhood I used to enjoy reading horror tales and had a desire to interview a ghost. I had a totally false understanding of ghosts till I heard your real-life experiences encountering ghosts and by now there is no attempt in your thoughts also to come across an evil spirit.

When You healed me and my family, I felt some channel was incomplete, was not feeling contented, and was restless thinking you have done so much for me and my family and I could not offer You anything in return as you refused to accept anything. In Vizag retreat, Guruji clearly told you, from now onwards not to heal anyone for free and I thanked Guruji since He answered my prayer. I was literally dancing in joy and Guruji happily tapped on my head and went.

I remember Guruji reminding You on the same, this Feb. He told You, "If You heal for free and do not accept in return, the person will not get the complete benefit. You can decide what to charge or Nature will guide You."

Testimonial

Feel very good to read Sruthi. You spread joy, positivity, and hope and by sharing your experiences you reinforce faith & trust in Divine and all that lies beyond this mundane world. You entice us into continuing our spiritual practices for the rewards of bliss that lie yonder.

Whether it's Devi Ma or Mary Ma, it's the same mother who is ever kind & gracious to her children. Thank you Sruthi for sharing your beautiful & out of the world experiences. May all be healthy & peaceful.

Testimonial

It was very nice to read about your experience Sruthi. Earlier out of ignorance when something wouldn't work in my favour, I used to blame the influence of Shani in a derogatory way. After a few years, I understood that Shani Dev is one who puts one on the right path by creating difficulties & problems. My obeisance to Him.

Again a few years ago, I was curious about the future, I requested a known astrologer to see my horoscope. He declined saying that one who is under the protection of a Guru need not worry about planetary influences. Sruthi, you are a Divine Being, a jewel among mortals.

Testimonial

Tears fill my eyes as I absorb the immense depth and unthinkable nature of the experiences you share. Your experiences act as a powerful catalyst, igniting awakening within.

Testimonial

Sruthi, your ability to transcend your emotions and demonstrate unconditional love for everyone is truly inspiring. The purity of mind you have attained is clearly guiding you to higher levels of consciousness.

Testimonial

Sruthi, I am in tears as I read about your incredible kindness. I am amazed at how you can extend such compassion even to those who have troubled you or betrayed you. Your ability to accept and still help those who have wronged you is truly divine. You embody the essence of divinity.

Testimonial

Sruthi, you are truly brave and courageous. It seems that all your problems are bound to fade away, knowing they can never win against you. You are a true fighter—hats off to you.

Om Shanti

Testimonial

Sruthi, despite everything you've been through, you have retained your smile and continued to inspire me and so many others.

Testimonial

Sruthi, your messages are always inspiring. They help me grow and change for the better, even if it's in small ways. Thank you, Sruthi.

Testimonial

Sruthi, you are truly divine. Just knowing that you are there for me brings a sense of relaxation and peace, even though I haven't been able to talk to you directly as I wished. I feel that you have already done something wonderful for me, and this peace I feel for no apparent reason means the world to me.

Thank you for everything, you have no idea how much this means to me.

Testimonial

Shruti, I wanted to share some good things about my sister's daughter. After your blessings on her, she is healthy and got visa to USA for studies.

Testimonial

Hi Dear, my BP is under control and now I don't take any medicine. Once again Thank you for everything, dear.

My Path as a Spiritual Guru

If I reflect on my life so far, I feel that I am blessed to come this way. I had my set of challenges.

I feel one should be grateful to everyone who helps us in our journey. I have lived my life with love and gratitude and will continue to do so. I went through unbearable situations, but never had self-pity, nor did I glorify myself.

Many of our meditation group members sought guidance from me after my Guru initiated me into the first Kundalini meditation level. This went on. I completed my second-level initiation. Later on, our meditation group members started requesting me to accept them as disciples; some more people who didn't belong to our group requested the same. I sought my Guru's guidance. He happily gave me his blessings to go ahead. Thus, my journey as a Guru began. I initiated a few students, and they are doing great; many people are still waiting to be initiated by me.

Professionally, I began my journey as a teacher, and it continues as a spiritual teacher.

After many years of practice of Kundalini Meditation, and raising my Kundalini several times, My Guru gave me his blessings to be a Guru and initiate students into Kundalini Meditation.

Practices for Transforming Life

Many aspire to become my disciple, but true strength lies in self-improvement. I guide individuals on the path of righteousness by teaching practical ways to grow and evolve. Transformation begins with small, mindful changes. Let me share a few powerful practices that can help you strengthen your journey and unlock your true potential:

1. Try to reduce your ego. The ego is the biggest hindrance to our spiritual growth once that diminishes, we progress.

2. Once we are done with ego, acceptance is possible, and with that unconditional love and positivity come, which are very important for our development.

3. Life becomes easier once we start accepting things as they are.

4. Accept your mistakes.

5. Forgive (all those who have hurt you) and let go. If possible, seek forgiveness and move on.

6. Let go of the past (this means, memories remain without affecting you anymore).

7. Don't have many plans for the future (The reason is, if things don't happen as you had planned, there will be pain, frustration, anger, and so on).

8. Live in the present moment.

9. Be contented, and having fewer desires makes life easy.

10. Analyse things before reacting or making decisions.

11. Try to be peaceful, no matter what comes your way. We can be peaceful when we accept everything positively.

12. Be positive always. Let your thoughts and actions be positive.

13. Try not to complain.

14. Try not to compare one's progress with others (it will cause hurt and jealousy).

15. Try not to force your opinion on others. Respect their thoughts.

16. Problems are an inevitable part of life and should be faced gracefully. Acceptance involves understanding and respecting others' thoughts, feelings, and experiences while recognizing that not everything is within our control. It does not mean tolerating injustice, complacency, or mediocrity, nor bowing down to wrongdoings or manipulative demands. Upholding values, integrity, and self-respect is crucial, even in adversity.

    Standing up for oneself, asserting boundaries, and expressing beliefs with courage are both self-preserving and a moral responsibility to deter negativity. True strength lies in saying 'no' when needed, discerning right from wrong, and addressing challenges constructively. This balanced approach fosters self-respect, earns others' respect, and sets a positive example of courage and integrity.

17. Each person's perception would be different. Never try to pull anyone down. Let our love be unconditional, pure, and free-flowing towards all.

18. Let's spread love, peace, positivity, and happiness wherever we go. Let there be no room for hatred, jealousy, comparison, superiority complex, gossip, or bad thoughts. We should not differentiate. Our love should be the same for all.

19. Don't envy; learn to appreciate the good in others. See the good in everything.

20. Try not to use harsh words. Do not insult or speak rudely to anyone.

21. Do not judge, or talk badly about others.

22. Don't hold a grudge towards anyone. Don't seek revenge; leave the past and live in the present (today).

23. Be loving and kind to everyone you meet in your life.

24. Have compassion and endurance, think good, and do good for all.

25. Do not differentiate between our own and others; treat everyone equally.

26. Be humble always. Lead a simple life.

27. Do your duty towards your own.

28. Help the needy, sick, and old. Do good things silently.

29. We must try to give back to Nature for the infinite blessings that we receive. Help the needy (the right ones; we will be shown who deserves help).

30. Do your best in all fields of life, without any expectations. You get what you deserve or what is meant for you.

31. Happily, accept and be grateful for what you receive from Nature. Each one's journey is different; do your part without expectations.

32. Meditation gives us answers. When we start following Divine Guidance, 100% of our weaknesses will be shown to us. We should constantly try to correct ourselves, making our weaknesses our strengths.

33. Nature truly helps; we are tested. Don't give up. Be patient. Keep smiling. Protect and respect Mother Nature. Plant trees.

34. Practice detachment. Accepting things as they are makes it much easier to handle many situations.

35. Offer gratitude to your Gurus, all Divine, Mother Earth, and the Universe.

Offering gratitude from the heart makes a person humble and breaks the ego. Offering gratitude from the heart is a profound act beyond mere words or gestures. When you genuinely express gratitude, you acknowledge that the blessings in your life—whether they come from others, nature, or a higher power—are not solely of your own making. This realization fosters humility, shifting your perspective from self-centeredness to interconnectedness.

In essence, offering gratitude from the heart is a practice of surrender. It invites you to bow before the larger forces at play in your life, whether they are people, circumstances, or divine guidance. This surrender doesn't diminish you; instead, it elevates you, freeing you from the weight of ego and filling you with the lightness of humility and grace.

PRIDE HAS A FALL. BE KIND ALWAYS.